Ancient Hebrew Dictionary

Cover design by Jeff A. Benner.

"Ancient Hebrew Dictionary," by Jeff A. Benner. ISBN 978-1-60264-377-2

Published 2009 by Virtualbookworm.com Publishing Inc., P.O. Box 9949, College Station, TX 77845, US.

Manufactured in the United States of America.

Ancient Hebrew Dictionary

1000 Verbs and Nouns of the Hebrew Bible

עַל פְּנֵי הַמָּיִם׃ וַיֹּאמֶר
הָאוֹר כִּי טוֹב וַיַּבְדֵּל אֱלֹהִים בֵּין הָאוֹר
יוֹם וְלַחֹשֶׁךְ קָרָא לָיְלָה וַיְהִי עֶרֶב וַיְהִי בֹקֶר
בְּתוֹךְ הַמָּיִם וִיהִי מַבְדִּיל בֵּין מַיִם לָמָיִם׃
הַמַּיִם אֲשֶׁר מִתַּחַת לָרָקִיעַ וּבֵין הַמַּיִם אֲשֶׁר
לָרָקִיעַ שָׁמָיִם וַיְהִי עֶרֶב וַיְהִי בֹקֶר יוֹם שֵׁנִי
הַשָּׁמַיִם אֶל מָקוֹם אֶחָד וְתֵרָאֶה
וּלְמִקְוֵה הַמַּיִם קָרָא יַמִּים וַיַּרְא

By Jeff A. Benner

To Jack and Jamie Waid, our good friends who are an inspiration to my wife and I and too many others.

Table of Contents

Introduction

About the Book

This book has been designed to be a quick reference guide for looking up the meaning of common Hebrew words found in the Hebrew Bible, as well as a resource for learning the Hebrew vocabulary.

Within this book is a list of the 1000 most frequently used Hebrew verbs (379) and nouns (621) from the Hebrew Bible. Each word entry includes:

1. The Hebrew word (in modern and ancient script).
2. A transliteration of the Hebrew word.
3. A one or two word translation of the Hebrew word.
4. A more detailed definition of the Hebrew word.
5. Cross references to other resources.

In the appendices are additional words and details about the Hebrew language including:

1. The Hebrew alphabet and vowels.
2. Hebrew prefixes and suffixes.

3. Pronouns, prepositions, etc.

4. Hebrew numbers.

5. Hebrew verb conjugations.

Dictionary Format

Below is an example entry, followed by an explanation of its contents.

944. שָׁלוֹם / 𐤔𐤋𐤅𐤌 / sha-lom **Translation:** Completeness **Definition:** Something that has been finished or made whole. A state of being complete. **AHLB:** 2845 (c) **Strong's:** 7965

Modern Hebrew Word

Following the entry number is the Hebrew word written in the Modern Hebrew script (שָׁלוֹם).

Ancient Hebrew Word

Each word is also written in the ancient pictographic script (𐤔𐤋𐤅𐤌). In some cases, this spelling may be different than the modern script. As an example, the word אֹהֶל (#390) includes the hholam vowel pointing (the dot above the aleph representing the "o" sound), but in most ancient documents this word is written as אוהל (where the letter vav represents the "o" sound) or 𐤀𐤅𐤄𐤋 in the ancient script. In addition, the spelling of words evolve over time. For instance, the word בּוֹר

(#452, bor, a cistern) comes from the root כור (kor) meaning "to dig a hole." Therefore, the ancient spelling of this word would have been כור (kor).

Transliteration

A transliteration from Hebrew into Roman letters (sha-lom) is given to assist with the pronunciation of Hebrew nouns. Verb transliterations will be represented by the consonants only. For instance, the transliteration for the Hebrew verb בדל (#20) is B.D.L.

Translation

This is one or two English words that best translate the Hebrew word. In many cases, this translation will be significantly different from what is found in other dictionaries. For instance, the word שָׁלוֹם is usually translated as "peace," but this abstract idea does not completely convey the original Hebraic meaning of this word. In this dictionary, the translation of this word is "Completeness." An index at the end of this book allows for a cross referencing from the English translation to its corresponding entry within this dictionary.

Definition

This is a more specific meaning of the word which reflects its textual and original Hebraic cultural perspective. As an example, in our culture, the word "peace" means "a state of mutual harmony between people or groups." However, in Biblical Hebrew, this word means "a state of being complete."

Cross References

Each entry includes a cross reference to the *Ancient Hebrew Lexicon of the Bible* and *Strong's Dictionary*. An index at the end of this book allows for a cross referencing from Strong's number to its corresponding entry within this dictionary.

Dictionary ~ Verbs

Aleph

1. אבד / 𐤀𐤁𐤃 / A.B.D **Translation:** Perish **Definition:** To be separated from the whole, life or functionality. **AHLB:** 1027-C (V) **Strong's:** 6

2. אבה / 𐤀𐤁𐤄 / A.B.H **Translation:** Consent **Definition:** To give approval; to be in concord in opinion or sentiment; agreement as to action or opinion; to be willing to go somewhere or do something. **AHLB:** 1028-C (V) **Strong's:** 14

3. אבל / 𐤀𐤁𐤋 / A.B.L **Translation:** Mourn **Definition:** To feel or express grief or sorrow. **AHLB:** 1035-C (V) **Strong's:** 56

4. אהב / 𐤀𐤄𐤁 / A.H.B **Translation:** Love **Definition:** To provide and protect that which is given as a privilege. An intimacy of action and emotion. Strong affection for another arising from personal ties. **AHLB:** 1094-C (V) **Strong's:** 157

More about the word אהב

We do not choose our parents or siblings, but are instead given to us as a gift from above, a privileged gift. Even in the ancient Hebrew culture ones wife was chosen. It is our responsibility to provide and protect that privileged gift. In our modern Western culture love is an abstract thought of emotion, how one feels toward another but the Hebrew meaning goes much deeper. As a verb this word means "to provide and protect what is given as a privilege" as well as " to have an intimacy of action and emotion". We are told to love Elohiym and our neighbors, not in an emotional sense, but in the sense of our actions.

5. אוה / 𐤀𐤅𐤄 / A.W.H **Translation:** Yearn **Definition:** To have an earnest or strong desire; long. **AHLB:** 1005-J (V) **Strong's:** 183

6. אור / 𐤀𐤅𐤓 / A.W.R **Translation:** Light **Definition:** To shine with an intense light; be or give off light; to be bright. **AHLB:** 1020-J (V) **Strong's:** 215

7. אזן / 𐤀𐤆𐤍 / A.Z.N **Translation:** Give an ear **Definition:** To pay attention to a voice or sound; to hear with thoughtful attention and obedience. **AHLB:** 1152-C (V) **Strong's:** 238

8. אחז / 𐤀𐤇𐤆 / A.Hh.Z **Translation:** Take hold **Definition:** To have possession or ownership of; to keep in restraint; to have or maintain in one's grasp; to grab something and keep hold of it. **AHLB:** 1168-C (V) **Strong's:** 270

9. איב / 𐤀𐤉𐤁 / A.Y.B **Translation:** Attack **Definition:** To be antagonistic or unfriendly to another. An action taken by an enemy. **AHLB:** 1002-M (V) **Strong's:** 341

10. אכל / 𐤀𐤊𐤋 / A.K.L **Translation:** Eat **Definition:** To consume food; to destroy. A devouring of a fire. **AHLB:** 1242-C (V) **Strong's:** 398

11. אמן / אמן / A.M.N **Translation:** Be firm **Definition:** Securely or solidly fixed in place; to stand firm in the sense of a support. Not subject to change or revision. The hiphil (causative) form means "support." **AHLB:** 1290-C (V) **Strong's:** 539

12. אמץ / אמץ / A.M.Ts **Translation:** Be strong **Definition:** To be mentally astute, firm, obstinate or courageous. Having or marked by great physical, moral or intellectual power. **AHLB:** 1294-C (V) **Strong's:** 553

13. אמר / אמר / A.M.R **Translation:** Say **Definition:** To speak chains of words that form sentences. **AHLB:** 1288-C (V) **Strong's:** 559

14. אסף / אסף / A.S.P **Translation:** Gather **Definition:** To bring together; to accumulate and place in readiness. **AHLB:** 1339-C (V) **Strong's:** 622

15. אסר / אסר / A.S.R **Translation:** Tie up **Definition:** To wrap or fasten with a cord. **AHLB:** 1342-C (V) **Strong's:** 631

16. אפה / אפה / A.P.H **Translation:** Bake **Definition:** To cook using dry heat, especially in an oven. **AHLB:** 1017-H (V) **Strong's:** 644

17. ארב / ארב / A.R.B **Translation:** Ambush **Definition:** To lay in wait of another to capture or do harm or injury. **AHLB:** 1439-C (V) **Strong's:** 693

18. ארך / ארך / A.R.K **Translation:** Prolong **Definition:** To lengthen or delay. **AHLB:** 1448-C (V) **Strong's:** 748

19. ארר / A.R.R **Translation:** Spit upon **Definition:** To eject saliva, usually on another in spite or disrespect. **AHLB:** 1457-C (V) **Strong's:** 779

20. אשׁם / A.Sh.M **Translation:** Be guilty **Definition:** To commit an offense, especially consciously. **AHLB:** 1473-C (V) **Strong's:** 816

Beyt

21. בגד / B.G.D **Translation:** Act treacherously **Definition:** To perform an action covertly or with the intent to deceive. **AHLB:** 2004 (V) **Strong's:** 898

22. בדל / B.D.L **Translation:** Separate **Definition:** To set or keep apart. **AHLB:** 2005 (V) **Strong's:** 914

23. בהל / B.H.L **Translation:** Stir **Definition:** To disturb the quiet of; agitate. **AHLB:** 1035-G (V) **Strong's:** 926

24. בוא / B.W.A **Translation:** Come **Definition:** To move toward something; approach; enter. This can be understood as to come or to go. The hiphil (causative) form means "bring." **AHLB:** 1024-J (V) **Strong's:** 935

25. בוש / B.W.Sh **Translation:** Be ashamed **Definition:** Feeling shame, guilt or disgrace; to be dried up with shame. **AHLB:** 1044-J (V) **Strong's:** 954

26. בזה / B.Z.H **Translation:** Disdain **Definition:** A feeling of contempt for what is beneath one; to look with scorn on; to treat something as spoiled or no longer of value. **AHLB:** 1030-H (V) **Strong's:** 959

27. בזז / / B.Z.Z **Translation:** Plunder **Definition:** To commit robbery or looting. **AHLB:** 1030-B (V) **Strong's:** 962

28. בחן / / B.Hh.N **Translation:** Examine **Definition:** To inspect closely; to test, try or scrutinize. **AHLB:** 2011 (V) **Strong's:** 974

29. בחר / / B.Hh.R **Translation:** Choose **Definition:** To select freely and after consideration. **AHLB:** 2012 (V) **Strong's:** 977

30. בטח / / B.Th.Hh **Translation:** Cling **Definition:** To grab a hold of someone or something that is secure and safe. **AHLB:** 2013 (V) **Strong's:** 982

31. בין / / B.Y.N **Translation:** Understand **Definition:** To grasp the meaning of; to have comprehension. **AHLB:** 1037-M (V) **Strong's:** 995

32. בכה / / B.K.H **Translation:** Weep **Definition:** To express deep sorrow, especially by shedding tears. **AHLB:** 1034-H (V) **Strong's:** 1058

33. בלל / / B.L.L **Translation:** Mix **Definition:** To combine in one mass; to mingle together. **AHLB:** 1035-B (V) **Strong's:** 1101

34. בלע / / B.L.Ah **Translation:** Swallow **Definition:** To pass through the mouth and move into the esophagus to the stomach. **AHLB:** 2020 (V) **Strong's:** 1104

35. בנה / / B.N.H **Translation:** Build **Definition:** To construct a building, home or family. **AHLB:** 1037-H (V) **Strong's:** 1129

36. בער / / B.Ah.R **Translation:** Burn **Definition:** To undergo rapid combustion or consume fuel in such a way as to give off heat, gases, and, usually, light; be on fire. **AHLB:** 2028 (V) **Strong's:** 1197

37. בצר / / B.Ts.R **Translation:** Fence in **Definition:** A barrier intended to protect, prevent escape or intrusion, or to mark a boundary; to gather together and confine for protection. **AHLB:** 2033 (V) **Strong's:** 1219

38. בקע / / B.Q.Ah **Translation:** Cleave **Definition:** To divide by or as if by a cutting blow; to separate into distinct parts; to break, cut or divide something in half. **AHLB:** 2034 (V) **Strong's:** 1234

39. בקש / / B.Q.Sh **Translation:** Search out **Definition:** To intently look for someone or something until the object of the search is found. **AHLB:** 2036 (V) **Strong's:** 1245

40. ברא / / B.R.A **Translation:** Fatten **Definition:** To make more substantial, fleshy or plump; to fill up. The filling of the earth in Genesis 1 with the sun, moon, plants and animals. The filling of man with breath and the image of Elohiym. **AHLB:** 1043-E (V) **Strong's:** 1254

41. ברח / / B.R.Hh **Translation:** Flee away **Definition:** To run away from. **AHLB:** 2038 (V) **Strong's:** 1272

42. ברך / [illegible] / B.R.K **Translation:** Kneel **Definition:** To bend the knee, to kneel in homage or to drink water. The piel (intensive) form means "respect," in the sense of kneeling before another. **AHLB:** 2039 (V) **Strong's:** 1288

More about the word ברך

The Hebrew verb barak means to kneel as seen in Genesis 24:11. However, when written in the piel form it means to show respect (usually translated as bless) as seen in Genesis 12:2. A related Hebrew word is berakhah meaning a gift or present. From this we can see the concrete meaning behind the piel form of the verb barak. It is to bring a gift to another while kneeling out of respect. The extended meaning of this word is to do or give something of value to another. Elohiym "respects" us by providing for our needs and we in turn "respect" Elohiym by giving him of ourselves as his servants.

43. בשׁל / [illegible] / B.Sh.L **Translation:** Boil **Definition:** To generate bubbles of vapor when heated; to cook a meat in water. The hiphil (causative) form means "ripen." **AHLB:** 2043 (V) **Strong's:** 1310

Gimel

44. גאל / [illegible] / G.A.L **Translation:** Redeem **Definition:** To buy back. Restore one to his original position or avenge his death. In the participle form this verb means "avenger," as it is the role of the nearest relative to buy back one in slavery or avenge his murder. **AHLB:** 1058-D (V) **Strong's:** 1350

45. גבה / / G.B.H **Translation:** Lift high **Definition:** To lift up to a greater elevation or stature. **AHLB:** 1048-H (V) **Strong's:** 1361

46. גבר / / G.B.R **Translation:** Overcome **Definition:** To get the better of. Be successful in strength or authority. **AHLB:** 2052 (V) **Strong's:** 1396

47. גדל / / G.D.L **Translation:** Magnify **Definition:** To increase in size or one's position of honor. **AHLB:** 2054 (V) **Strong's:** 1431

48. גור / / G.W.R **Translation:** Sojourn **Definition:** To stay as a temporary resident. Travel in a strange land. Also, the extended meaning of "to be afraid" of a stranger. **AHLB:** 1066-J (V) **Strong's:** 1481

49. גזל / / G.Z.L **Translation:** Pluck away **Definition:** To take off something or someone by force through picking off, robbing or plundering. **AHLB:** 2059 (V) **Strong's:** 1497

50. גיל / / G.Y.L **Translation:** Dance around **Definition:** To celebrate or rejoice by spinning or moving around in a circle. **AHLB:** 1058-M (V) **Strong's:** 1523

51. גלה / / G.L.H **Translation:** Remove the cover **Definition:** To reveal something by exposing it. Usually to be exposed from the removal of clothing. **AHLB:** 1357-H (V) **Strong's:** 1540

52. גמל / / G.M.L **Translation:** Yield **Definition:** To produce or be productive. **AHLB:** 2070 (V) **Strong's:** 1580

53. גנב / / G.N.B **Translation:** Steal **Definition:** To wrongfully take the property of another; rob. **AHLB:** 2073 (V) **Strong's:** 1589

54. גרש / / G.R.Sh **Translation:** Cast out **Definition:** To drive out, expel, thrust away. **AHLB:** 2089 (V) **Strong's:** 1644

Dalet

55. דבק / / D.B.Q **Translation:** Adhere **Definition:** To join or stick to someone or something. **AHLB:** 2092 (V) **Strong's:** 1692

56. דבר / / D.B.R **Translation:** Speak **Definition:** A careful arrangement of words or commands said orally. **AHLB:** 2093 (V) **Strong's:** 1696

57. דמה / / D.M.H **Translation:** Resemble **Definition:** To be like, similar or compared to something else. **AHLB:** 1082-H (V) **Strong's:** 1819

58. דרך / / D.R.K **Translation:** Step upon **Definition:** To take a step; to take a journey as a treading. The stringing of a bow through the idea of stepping the foot over the bow and using the leg to bend it. **AHLB:** 2112 (V) **Strong's:** 1869

59. דרש / / D.R.Sh **Translation:** Seek **Definition:** To look for or search for something or for answers. The niphal (passive) form means "require." **AHLB:** 2114 (V) **Strong's:** 1875

Hey

60. הגה / 𐤄𐤂𐤄 / H.G.H **Translation:** Mutter **Definition:** To moan or growl in deep meditation or mourning. **AHLB:** 1095-H (V) **Strong's:** 1897

61. היה / 𐤄𐤉𐤄 / H.Y.H **Translation:** Exist **Definition:** To have real being whether material or spiritual; to have breath. **AHLB:** 1097-M (V) **Strong's:** 1961

62. הלך / 𐤄𐤋𐤊 / H.L.K **Translation:** Walk **Definition:** To move along on foot; walk a journey; to go. Also, customs as a lifestyle that is walked or lived. **AHLB:** 1264-F (V) **Strong's:** 1980

63. הלל / 𐤄𐤋𐤋 / H.L.L **Translation:** Shine **Definition:** To emit rays of light. Shine brightly. To shine or cause another to shine through one's actions or words. The piel (intensive) form means "commend." **AHLB:** 1104-B (V) **Strong's:** 1984

More about the word הלל

The Hebrew verb halal means "to shine" as can be seen Job 29:3. But when it is written in its piel form it means "commend" (usually translated as "praise"). However, commend is an abstract word that must be understood through the ancient Hebrew's concrete way of thinking. The North Star, unlike all of the other stars, remains motionless and constantly shines in the northern sky and is used as a guide when traveling. In the Ancient Hebrew mind we praise Elohiym by looking at him as the guiding star that shines to show us our direction.

64. המה / / H.M.H **Translation:** Roar **Definition:** A loud noise as from the sea or a crowd. **AHLB:** 1105-H (V) **Strong's:** 1993

65. הפך / / H.P.K **Translation:** Overturn **Definition:** To turn something over or upside down, as if pouring out its contents. **AHLB:** 1379-F (V) **Strong's:** 2015

66. הרג / / H.R.G **Translation:** Kill **Definition:** To deprive of life; to slaughter. **AHLB:** 1440-F (V) **Strong's:** 2026

67. הרה / / H.R.H **Translation:** Conceive **Definition:** To become pregnant with young. **AHLB:** 1112-H (V) **Strong's:** 2029

68. הרס / / H.R.S **Translation:** Cast down **Definition:** To ruin or break into pieces by throwing or pulling down. **AHLB:** 1452-F (V) **Strong's:** 2040

Zayin

69. זבח / / Z.B.Hh **Translation:** Sacrifice **Definition:** An act of offering to deity something precious; to kill an animal for an offering. **AHLB:** 2117 (V) **Strong's:** 2076

70. זוב / 𐤆𐤅𐤁 / Z.W.B **Translation:** Issue **Definition:** To flow out; to go, pass, or flow out; emerge. **AHLB:** 1140-J (V) **Strong's:** 2100

71. זור / 𐤆𐤅𐤓 / Z.W.R **Translation:** Be strange **Definition:** To be separated out from others; to be scattered abroad. **AHLB:** 1158-J (V) **Strong's:** 2114

72. זכר / 𐤆𐤊𐤓 / Z.K.R **Translation:** Remember **Definition:** To bring to mind or think of again; to act or speak on behalf of another. Remember in thought as a memorial or mention through speech. The hiphil (causative) form means "mention." **AHLB:** 2121 (V) **Strong's:** 2142

73. זמר / 𐤆𐤌𐤓 / Z.M.R **Translation:** Pluck **Definition:** To make music by plucking an instrument. To pick fruit. **AHLB:** 2124 (V) **Strong's:** 2167

74. זנה / 𐤆𐤍𐤄 / Z.N.H **Translation:** Be a whore **Definition:** A woman who practices promiscuous sexual behavior, especially for hire. **AHLB:** 1152-H (V) **Strong's:** 2181

75. זעק / 𐤆𐤏𐤒 / Z.Ah.Q **Translation:** Yell out **Definition:** To call out in a louder than normal voice; to declare; to cry out for help. **AHLB:** 2131 (V) **Strong's:** 2199

76. זקן / 𐤆𐤒𐤍 / Z.Q.N **Translation:** Be old **Definition:** To be of an advanced age. **AHLB:** 2132 (V) **Strong's:** 2204

77. זרה / 𐤆𐤓𐤄 / Z.R.H **Translation:** Disperse **Definition:** To separate or remove to a distance apart from each other; to diffuse or cause to break into different parts. **AHLB:** 1158-H (V) **Strong's:** 2219

78. זרע / / Z.R.Ah **Translation:** Sow **Definition:** To spread seeds on the ground; to plant a crop. **AHLB:** 2137 (V) **Strong's:** 2232

79. זרק / / Z.R.Q **Translation:** Sprinkle **Definition:** To drip a liquid, usually water or blood. **AHLB:** 2138 (V) **Strong's:** 2236

Hhet

80. חבא / / Hh.B.A **Translation:** Withdraw **Definition:** To take back or withhold what is cherished; to turn away or move back. **AHLB:** 1163-E (V) **Strong's:** 2244

81. חבר / / Hh.B.R **Translation:** Couple **Definition:** To bind by joining or coupling together. **AHLB:** 2143 (V) **Strong's:** 2266

82. חבש / / Hh.B.Sh **Translation:** Saddle **Definition:** A shaped mounted support on which an object can travel; to bind up with a saddle. **AHLB:** 2144 (V) **Strong's:** 2280

83. חגר / / Hh.G.R **Translation:** Gird up **Definition:** To bind the loose portions of clothing into a belt or sash to prepare to go to war; to be bound with arms for war. **AHLB:** 2147 (V) **Strong's:** 2296

84. חדל / / Hh.D.L **Translation:** Terminate **Definition:** To stop or refrain from continuing an action. **AHLB:** 2148 (V) **Strong's:** 2308

85. חול / / Hh.W.L **Translation:** Twist **Definition:** A winding or wrapping together; entwined in pain or joy. **AHLB:** 1173-J (V) **Strong's:** 2342

86. חזה / / Hh.Z.H **Translation:** Perceive **Definition:** To be able to understand on a higher level; to see something that is not physically present. **AHLB:** 1168-H (V) **Strong's:** 2372

87. חזק / / Hh.Z.Q **Translation:** Seize **Definition:** To possess or take by force; grab hold tightly; to refrain or support by grabbing hold. **AHLB:** 2152 (V) **Strong's:** 2388

88. חטא / / Hh.Th.A **Translation:** Err **Definition:** To miss the target, whether a literal target or a goal that is aimed for. The piel (intensive) form means "reconcile." **AHLB:** 1170-E (V) **Strong's:** 2398

89. חיה / / Hh.Y.H **Translation:** Live **Definition:** To be alive and continue alive. Have life within. The revival of life gained from food or other necessity. The piel (intensive) form means "keep alive." **AHLB:** 1171-H (V) **Strong's:** 2421

90. חכם / / Hh.K.M **Translation:** Be skilled **Definition:** To be able to decide or discern between good and bad, right and wrong; to act correctly in thought and action. **AHLB:** 2159 (V) **Strong's:** 2449

91. חלה / / Hh.L.H **Translation:** Be sick **Definition:** To be twisted through pain. **AHLB:** 1173-H (V) **Strong's:** 2470

92. חלל / / Hh.L.L **Translation:** Pierce **Definition:** To run into or through as with a pointed weapon or tool; pierce a hole through; to begin in the sense of pressing in. **AHLB:** 1173-B (V) **Strong's:** 2490

93. חלם / Hh.L.M **Translation:** Visualize **Definition:** To see or form a mental image of; to dream dreams. **AHLB:** 2164 (V) **Strong's:** 2492

94. חלף / Hh.L.P **Translation:** Pass over **Definition:** To pass through, by or over something. Also, to change in the sense of going to another one, side or thought. The piel (intensive) form means "change." **AHLB:** 2165 (V) **Strong's:** 2498

95. חלץ / Hh.L.Ts **Translation:** Draw **Definition:** To pull out or toward. **AHLB:** 2166 (V) **Strong's:** 2502

96. חלק / Hh.L.Q **Translation:** Apportion **Definition:** To divide and mete out according to a plan among the appropriate recipients. **AHLB:** 2167 (V) **Strong's:** 2505

97. חמל / Hh.M.L **Translation:** Show pity **Definition:** To have compassion; to sympathize. **AHLB:** 2171 (V) **Strong's:** 2550

98. חנה / Hh.N.H **Translation:** Camp **Definition:** To erect temporary shelters (as tents) together; to stop for the night and pitch the tents. **AHLB:** 1175-H (V) **Strong's:** 2583

99. חנן / Hh.N.N **Translation:** Show beauty **Definition:** To give or show beauty, grace or mercy to another. The hitpael (reflexive) form means "beseech." **AHLB:** 1175-B (V) **Strong's:** 2603

100. חסה / / Hh.S.H **Translation:** Refuge **Definition:** To take shelter or place ones trust in someone or something of support. **AHLB:** 1176-H (V) **Strong's:** 2620

101. חפץ / / Hh.P.Ts **Translation:** Delight **Definition:** To desire something out of pleasure or necessity; to have a high degree of gratification. **AHLB:** 2191 (V) **Strong's:** 2654

102. חקר / / Hh.Q.R **Translation:** Examine **Definition:** To intently search or seek for details. **AHLB:** 2198 (V) **Strong's:** 2713

103. חרב / / Hh.R.B **Translation:** Dry up **Definition:** To be a dry wasteland; to be laid waste and made desolate. **AHLB:** 2199 (V) **Strong's:** 2717

104. חרד / / Hh.R.D **Translation:** Tremble **Definition:** To shake involuntarily; shiver. **AHLB:** 2201 (V) **Strong's:** 2729

105. חרה / / Hh.R.H **Translation:** Flare up **Definition:** To become suddenly excited or angry; to break out suddenly. Burn with a fierce anger. **AHLB:** 1181-H (V) **Strong's:** 2734

106. חרף / / Hh.R.P **Translation:** Taunt **Definition:** To pierce another with sharp words of reproach or scorn. **AHLB:** 2208 (V) **Strong's:** 2778

107. חרש / / Hh.R.Sh **Translation:** Scratch **Definition:** To plow in the sense of scratching a line in the soil; to engrave on wood or stone by scratching. This word can also mean "to hold in peace" or be silent. **AHLB:** 2211 (V) **Strong's:** 2790

108. חשב / 𐤇𐤔𐤁 / Hh.Sh.B **Translation:** Think **Definition:** To plan or design a course of action, item or invention. **AHLB:** 2213 (V) **Strong's:** 2803

109. חשך / 𐤇𐤔𐤊 / Hh.S.K **Translation:** Keep back **Definition:** To hold something back or restrain. **AHLB:** 2182 (V) **Strong's:** 2820

110. חתם / 𐤇𐤕𐤌 / Hh.T.M **Translation:** Seal **Definition:** To close tightly, often marked with the emblem of the owner that must be broken before opening. **AHLB:** 2223 (V) **Strong's:** 2856

111. חתן / 𐤇𐤕𐤍 / Hh.T.N **Translation:** Be an in-law **Definition:** To have a relationship with another through marriage. **AHLB:** 2224 (V) **Strong's:** 2859

112. חתת / 𐤇𐤕𐤕 / Hh.T.T **Translation:** Break **Definition:** To beat or shatter into pieces; to fear or be in terror in the sense of being shattered. **AHLB:** 1183-B (V) **Strong's:** 2865

Tet

113. טהר / 𐤈𐤄𐤓 / Th.H.R **Translation:** Be clean **Definition:** Free from dirt, pollution or immorality; unadulterated, pure. **AHLB:** 1204-G (V) **Strong's:** 2891

114. טוב / 𐤈𐤅𐤁 / Th.W.B **Translation:** Do good **Definition:** To act functionally. **AHLB:** 1186-J (V) **Strong's:** 2895

115. טמא / Th.M.A **Translation:** Be unclean **Definition:** Physically or morally impure; dirty, filthy. **AHLB:** 1197-E (V) **Strong's:** 2930

116. טמן / Th.M.N **Translation:** Submerge **Definition:** To hide by burying or to cover. **AHLB:** 2234 (V) **Strong's:** 2934

117. טרף / Th.R.P **Translation:** Tear into pieces **Definition:** To tear into pieces as a predator does to its prey; to rip a cloth into pieces. **AHLB:** 2245 (V) **Strong's:** 2963

Yud

118. יבש / Y.B.Sh **Translation:** Dry out **Definition:** To be dried up as well as withered, ashamed or confused. **AHLB:** 1044-L (V) **Strong's:** 3001

119. יגע / Y.G.Ah **Translation:** Weary **Definition:** To be tired from vigorous work. **AHLB:** 1062-L (V) **Strong's:** 3021

120. ידה / Y.D.H **Translation:** Throw the hand **Definition:** To stretch out the hand to grab; to show praise or confession. **AHLB:** 1211-H (V) **Strong's:** 3034

121. ידע / Y.D.Ah **Translation:** Know **Definition:** To have an intimate and personal understanding; to have an intimate relationship with another person. **AHLB:** 1085-L (V) **Strong's:** 3045

More about the word ידע

The idea of "knowing" in Ancient Hebrew thought is similar to our understanding of knowing but is more personal and intimate. We may say that we "know" someone but simply mean we "know" of his or her existence, but in Hebrew thought, one can only "know" someone if they have a personal and intimate relationship with them. In Genesis 18:19 Elohiym says about Abraham, "I know him" meaning he has a very close relationship with Abraham. In Genesis 4:1 it says that Adam "knew Eve his wife" implying a very intimate relationship.

122. יהב / 𐤉𐤄𐤁 / Y.H.B **Translation:** Provide **Definition:** To give what is due; to grant or allow permission. **AHLB:** 1094-L (V) **Strong's:** 3051

123. יחל / 𐤉𐤇𐤋 / Y.Hh.L **Translation:** Stay **Definition:** To remain behind; to wait in anticipation. **AHLB:** 1181-L (V) **Strong's:** 3176

124. יטב / 𐤉𐤈𐤁 / Y.Th.B **Translation:** Do well **Definition:** To do something necessary; to be good, in the sense of being "functional.". **AHLB:** 1186-L (V) **Strong's:** 3190

125. יכח / 𐤉𐤊𐤇 / Y.K.Hh **Translation:** Convict **Definition:** To find or prove to be guilty. **AHLB:** 1238-L (V) **Strong's:** 3198

126. יכל / 𐤉𐤊𐤋 / Y.K.L **Translation:** Be able **Definition:** To successfully prevail, overcome or endure. **AHLB:** 1242-L (V) **Strong's:** 3201

127. ילד / Y.L.D **Translation:** Bring forth **Definition:** To issue out; to bring forth children, either by the woman who bears them or the man who fathers them. The piel (intensive) form means "act-as-midwife." **AHLB:** 1257-L (V) **Strong's:** 3205

128. ילל / Y.L.L **Translation:** Howl **Definition:** To make a loud wail in grief or pain. **AHLB:** 1265-L (V) **Strong's:** 3213

129. ינח / Y.N.Hh **Translation:** Deposit **Definition:** To place, especially for safekeeping or as a pledge; to be laid down; to sit down to rest or remain in place. **AHLB:** 1307-L (V) **Strong's:** 3240

130. ינק / Y.N.Q **Translation:** Suckle **Definition:** To give milk to from the breast or udder. The hiphil (causative) form means "nurse (verb)." **AHLB:** 1318-L (V) **Strong's:** 3243

131. יסד / Y.S.D **Translation:** Found **Definition:** To lay a foundation of a house, place or plan. **AHLB:** 1326-L (V) **Strong's:** 3245

132. יסף / Y.S.P **Translation:** Add **Definition:** To augment something by increasing it in amount or supply. The hiphil (causative) form means "again." **AHLB:** 1339-L (V) **Strong's:** 3254

133. יסר / Y.S.R **Translation:** Correct **Definition:** To make a preferred change in direction through instruction or chastisement. **AHLB:** 1342-L (V) **Strong's:** 3256

134. יעד / Y.Ah.D **Translation:** Appoint **Definition:** To arrange, fix or set in place, to determine a set place or time to meet. **AHLB:** 1349-L (V) **Strong's:** 3259

135. יצא / Y.Ts.A **Translation:** Go out **Definition:** To go, come or issue forth. **AHLB:** 1392-L (V) **Strong's:** 3318

136. יצב / Y.Ts.B **Translation:** Station **Definition:** To stand firm and in place. **AHLB:** 1393-L (V) **Strong's:** 3320

137. יצק / Y.Ts.Q **Translation:** Pour down **Definition:** To send a liquid from a container into another container or onto a person or object; to pour molten metal into a cast. **AHLB:** 1410-L (V) **Strong's:** 3332

138. יצר / Y.Ts.R **Translation:** Mold **Definition:** To give shape to; to press or squeeze, as when pressing clay into a shape to form a vessel. **AHLB:** 1411-L (V) **Strong's:** 3335

139. יצת / Y.Ts.T **Translation:** Light on fire **Definition:** To kindle a blaze. **AHLB:** 1413-L (V) **Strong's:** 3341

140. ירא / Y.R.A **Translation:** Fear **Definition:** To be afraid of; to have a strong emotion caused by anticipation or awareness of danger; to dread what is terrible or revere what is respected. **AHLB:** 1227-E (V) **Strong's:** 3372

More about the word ירא

The root meaning of the word yara is "to flow" and is related to words meaning rain or stream as a flowing of water. In Hebrew thought fear can be what is felt when in danger or what is felt when in the presence of an awesome sight or person of great authority. These feelings flow out of the person through their actions, such as shaking when in fear or bowing down in awe of one in authority.

141. ירד / / Y.R.D **Translation:** Go down **Definition:** To go or come lower from a higher place. The hiphil (causative) form means "bring down." **AHLB:** 1441-L (V) **Strong's:** 3381

142. ירה / / Y.R.H **Translation:** Throw **Definition:** To propel through the air by a forward motion; to drizzle as a throwing down of water; to teach in the sense of throwing or pointing a finger in a straight line as the direction one is to walk. The hiphil (causative) form means "teach." **AHLB:** 1227-H (V) **Strong's:** 3384

143. ירש / / Y.R.Sh **Translation:** Possess **Definition:** To come into possession of or receive especially as a right or divine portion; o receive from an ancestor at his death; to take possession, either by seizing or through inheritance. **AHLB:** 1458-L (V) **Strong's:** 3423

144. ישב / / Y.Sh.B **Translation:** Settle **Definition:** To stay in a dwelling place for the night or for long periods of time; to sit down. **AHLB:** 1462-L (V) **Strong's:** 3427

145. ישע / / Y.Sh.Ah **Translation:** Rescue **Definition:** To free or deliver from a trouble, burden or danger. **AHLB:** 1476-L (V) **Strong's:** 3467

146. ישר / / Y.Sh.R **Translation:** Be straight **Definition:** To be in a direct or correct line, path or thought. **AHLB:** 1480-L (V) **Strong's:** 3474

147. יתר / / Y.T.R **Translation:** Leave behind **Definition:** To set aside; to retain or hold over to a future time or place; to leave a remainder. **AHLB:** 1480-L (V) **Strong's:** 3498

Kaph

148. כבד / 𐤊𐤁𐤃 / K.B.D **Translation:** Be heavy **Definition:** To be great in weight, wealth or importance. The piel (intensive) form means "honor." **AHLB:** 2246 (V) **Strong's:** 3513

149. כבס / 𐤊𐤁𐤎 / K.B.S **Translation:** Wash **Definition:** To immerse articles of clothing into a cleaning solution and agitate them, usually by treading upon them, to clean them; to clean the body. **AHLB:** 2249 (V) **Strong's:** 3526

150. כול / 𐤊𐤅𐤋 / K.W.L **Translation:** Sustain **Definition:** To provide what is needed to make someone or something whole or complete. **AHLB:** 1242-J (V) **Strong's:** 3557

151. כון / 𐤊𐤅𐤍 / K.W.N **Translation:** Prepare **Definition:** To put in proper condition or readiness. The piel (intensive) form means "establish." **AHLB:** 1244-J (V) **Strong's:** 3559

152. כחד / 𐤊𐤇𐤃 / K.Hh.D **Translation:** Keep secret **Definition:** To refrain from disclosing information. **AHLB:** 2255 (V) **Strong's:** 3582

153. כלה / 𐤊𐤋𐤄 / K.L.H **Translation:** Finish **Definition:** To bring to an end; terminate; to complete an action, event. **AHLB:** 1242-H (V) **Strong's:** 3615

154. כלם / כלם / K.L.M **Translation:** Shame **Definition:** To feel pain through something dishonorable, improper or ridiculous. **AHLB:** 2261 (V) **Strong's:** 3637

155. כנע / כנע / K.N.Ah **Translation:** Lower **Definition:** To be brought down low in humility or submission. **AHLB:** 2268 (V) **Strong's:** 3665

156. כסה / כסה / K.S.H **Translation:** Cover over **Definition:** To prevent disclosure or recognition of; to place out of sight; to completely cover over or hide. **AHLB:** 1245-H (V) **Strong's:** 3680

157. כעס / כעס / K.Ah.S **Translation:** Anger **Definition:** A strong feeling of displeasure and belligerence aroused by a wrong. **AHLB:** 2279 (V) **Strong's:** 3707

158. כפר / כפר / K.P.R **Translation:** Cover **Definition:** To afford protection or security; to hide from sight or knowledge; to cover over as with a lid. **AHLB:** 2283 (V) **Strong's:** 3722

More about the word כפר

The Hebrew word kaphar means "to cover over," but is often translated as atonement. The word atonement is an abstract word and in order to understand the true Hebrew meaning of a word we must look to the concrete meaning. If an offense has been made, the one that has been offended can act as though the offense is covered over and unseen. We express this idea through the word of forgiveness. Atonement is an outward action that covers over the error.

159. כרע / 𐤊𐤓𐤏 / K.R.Ah **Translation:** Stoop **Definition:** To bend the body forward and downward while bending the knees; to stoop or crouch down by bending or getting on the knees. **AHLB:** 2290 (V) **Strong's:** 3766

160. כרת / 𐤊𐤓𐤕 / K.R.T **Translation:** Cut **Definition:** To penetrate with a sharp edged instrument. **AHLB:** 2291 (V) **Strong's:** 3772

161. כשל / 𐤊𐤔𐤋 / K.Sh.L **Translation:** Topple **Definition:** To fall over in death or from being pushed. **AHLB:** 2292 (V) **Strong's:** 3782

162. כתב / 𐤊𐤕𐤁 / K.T.B **Translation:** Write **Definition:** To describe one's thoughts or instruction in a form that is readable. **AHLB:** 2295 (V) **Strong's:** 3789

Lamed

163. לבש / 𐤋𐤁𐤔 / L.B.Sh **Translation:** Wear **Definition:** To cover with cloth or clothing; to provide with clothing; put on clothing. The hiphil (causative) form means "clothe." **AHLB:** 2304 (V) **Strong's:** 3847

164. לוה / 𐤋𐤅𐤄 / L.W.H **Translation:** Join **Definition:** To bind together. **AHLB:** 1259-J (V) **Strong's:** 3867

165. לון / 𐤋𐤅𐤍 / L.W.N **Translation:** Stay the night **Definition:** To remain or stay through the night. **AHLB:** 1267-J (V) **Strong's:** 3885

166. לוץ / L.W.Ts **Translation:** Mimic **Definition:** To imitate another person-s speech as an interpretation or in scorn. **AHLB:** 1271-J (V) **Strong's:** 3887

167. לחם / L.Hh.M **Translation:** Fight **Definition:** To make war; to battle as to destruction; to attempt to defeat, subdue, or destroy an enemy by blows or weapons. A struggle for victory. **AHLB:** 2305 (V) **Strong's:** 3898

168. לכד / L.K.D **Translation:** Capture **Definition:** To forcefully take or seize. **AHLB:** 2310 (V) **Strong's:** 3920

169. למד / L.M.D **Translation:** Learn **Definition:** To acquire knowledge or skill through instruction from one who is experienced. **AHLB:** 2311 (V) **Strong's:** 3925

170. לקח / L.Q.Hh **Translation:** Take **Definition:** To receive what is given; to gain possession by seizing. **AHLB:** 2319 (V) **Strong's:** 3947

171. לקט / L.Q.Th **Translation:** Pick up **Definition:** To take hold of and lift up; to gather together. **AHLB:** 2320 (V) **Strong's:** 3950

Mem

172. מאן / M.A.N **Translation:** Refuse **Definition:** To express one's self as being unwilling to accept. **AHLB:** 1290-D (V) **Strong's:** 3985

173. מאס / [illegible] / M.A.S **Translation:** Reject **Definition:** To refuse an action or thought that is not wanted or is despised. **AHLB:** 1291-D (V) **Strong's:** 3988

174. מדד / [illegible] / M.D.D **Translation:** Measure **Definition:** To determine the length of something by comparing it to a standard of measure. **AHLB:** 1280-B (V) **Strong's:** 4058

175. מהר / [illegible] / M.H.R **Translation:** Hurry **Definition:** To carry or cause to go with haste. **AHLB:** 1296-G (V) **Strong's:** 4116

176. מוט / [illegible] / M.W.Th **Translation:** Shake **Definition:** To waver as a green branch. **AHLB:** 1285-J (V) **Strong's:** 4131

177. מול / [illegible] / M.W.L **Translation:** Circumcise **Definition:** To cut off the foreskin of a male. **AHLB:** 1288-J (V) **Strong's:** 4135

178. מות / [illegible] / M.W.T **Translation:** Die **Definition:** To pass from physical life; to pass out of existence; to come to an end through death. The hiphil (causative) form means "kill." **AHLB:** 1298-J (V) **Strong's:** 4191

179. מחה / [illegible] / M.Hh.H **Translation:** Wipe away **Definition:** To remove by drying or sweeping away through rubbing; to polish in the sense of a vigorous rubbing; erase. **AHLB:** 1284-H (V) **Strong's:** 4229

180. מכר / [illegible] / M.K.R **Translation:** Sell **Definition:** To give up property to another for money or another valuable compensation. **AHLB:** 2337 (V) **Strong's:** 4376

181. מלא / 𐤌𐤋𐤀 / M.L.A **Translation:** Fill **Definition:** To occupy to the full capacity. The piel (intensive) form means "fulfill." **AHLB:** 1288-E (V) **Strong's:** 4390

182. מלט / 𐤌𐤋𐤈 / M.L.Th **Translation:** Slip away **Definition:** To get away through deliverance or escape. **AHLB:** 2339 (V) **Strong's:** 4422

183. מלך / 𐤌𐤋𐤊 / M.L.K **Translation:** Reign **Definition:** To rule over a kingdom as king or queen. **AHLB:** 2340 (V) **Strong's:** 4427

184. מנה / 𐤌𐤍𐤄 / M.N.H **Translation:** Reckon **Definition:** To appoint, assign, count or number a set of things or people. **AHLB:** 1290-H (V) **Strong's:** 4487

185. מנע / 𐤌𐤍𐤏 / M.N.Ah **Translation:** Withhold **Definition:** To hold back from action. **AHLB:** 2343 (V) **Strong's:** 4513

186. מעל / 𐤌𐤏𐤋 / M.Ah.L **Translation:** Transgress **Definition:** To commit an unintentional or treacherous act that results in error. **AHLB:** 2349 (V) **Strong's:** 4603

187. מצא / 𐤌𐤑𐤀 / M.Ts.A **Translation:** Find **Definition:** To come upon, often accidentally; to meet with; to discover and secure through searching. **AHLB:** 1294-E (V) **Strong's:** 4672

188. מרד / 𐤌𐤓𐤃 / M.R.D **Translation:** Rebel **Definition:** To oppose or disobey one in authority or control. **AHLB:** 2352 (V) **Strong's:** 4775

189. מרה / / M.R.H **Translation:** Bitter **Definition:** Having a harsh, disagreeably acrid taste; to be rebellious or disobedient. **AHLB:** 1296-H (V) **Strong's:** 4784

190. משח / / M.Sh.Hh **Translation:** Smear **Definition:** To overspread with oil for medical treatment or as a sign of authority. **AHLB:** 2357 (V) **Strong's:** 4886

191. משך / / M.Sh.K **Translation:** Draw **Definition:** To pull up or out of a receptacle or place; to draw or pull something out; to prolong in the sense of drawing out time; to draw out a sound from a horn. **AHLB:** 2358 (V) **Strong's:** 4900

192. משל / / M.Sh.L **Translation:** Regulate **Definition:** To govern or correct according to rule; to bring order, method, or uniformity to; to compare one thing to another in the sense of a rule of measurement, often as a proverb or parable. **AHLB:** 2359 (V) **Strong's:** 4910

Nun

193. נאף / / N.A.P **Translation:** Commit adultery **Definition:** To perform voluntary violation of the marriage bed. **AHLB:** 2365 (V) **Strong's:** 5003

194. נבא / / N.B.A **Translation:** Prophecy **Definition:** To utter the words or instructions of Elohiym received through a vision or dream. **AHLB:** 1301-E (V) **Strong's:** 5012

195. נבט / 𐤍𐤁𐤈 / N.B.Th **Translation:** Stare **Definition:** To carefully look; to make a close inspection. **AHLB:** 2367 (V) **Strong's:** 5027

196. נגד / 𐤍𐤂𐤃 / N.G.D **Translation:** Be face to face **Definition:** To face another. The hiphil (causative) form means "tell" in the sense of speaking face to face. **AHLB:** 2372 (V) **Strong's:** 5046

197. נגע / 𐤍𐤂𐤏 / N.G.Ah **Translation:** Touch **Definition:** To lay hands upon; to touch or strike; to be touched by a plague. **AHLB:** 2376 (V) **Strong's:** 5060

198. נגף / 𐤍𐤂𐤐 / N.G.P **Translation:** Smite **Definition:** To deliver a hit with the intent to harm; to bring a plague in the sense of a striking. **AHLB:** 2377 (V) **Strong's:** 5062

199. נגש / 𐤍𐤂𐤔 / N.G.Sh **Translation:** Draw near **Definition:** To bring close to another. **AHLB:** 2379 (V) **Strong's:** 5066

200. נדד / 𐤍𐤃𐤃 / N.D.D **Translation:** Toss **Definition:** To heave or fling about; to throw with a quick, light, or careless motion; to be thrown about or wander around as nodding the head. **AHLB:** 1303-B (V) **Strong's:** 5074

201. נדח / 𐤍𐤃𐤇 / N.D.Hh **Translation:** Drive **Definition:** To forcefully send someone or something out or away; to drive an axe through wood. **AHLB:** 2381 (V) **Strong's:** 5080

202. נדר / 𐤍𐤃𐤓 / N.D.R **Translation:** Make a vow **Definition:** To promise solemnly; to make an agreement where one promises an action if the other reciprocates with another action. **AHLB:** 2385 (V) **Strong's:** 5087

203. נהג / 𐤍𐤄𐤂 / N.H.G **Translation:** Drive **Definition:** To set or keep in motion; to press or force into an activity, course, or direction. **AHLB:** 1302-G (V) **Strong's:** 5090

204. נוח / 𐤍𐤅𐤇 / N.W.Hh **Translation:** Rest **Definition:** Freedom from activity or labor. To rest from trouble or labor. **AHLB:** 1307-J (V) **Strong's:** 5117

205. נוס / 𐤍𐤅𐤎 / N.W.S **Translation:** Flee **Definition:** To run away, often from danger or evil; to hurry toward a place of safety; to flee to any safe place such as a city or mountain. **AHLB:** 1314-J (V) **Strong's:** 5127

206. נוע / 𐤍𐤅𐤏 / N.W.Ah **Translation:** Stagger **Definition:** To reel from side to side; to wag or shake back and forth or up and down; to wander as staggering about. **AHLB:** 1322-J (V) **Strong's:** 5128

207. נוף / 𐤍𐤅𐤐 / N.W.P **Translation:** Wave **Definition:** To move an object, such as hammer or a sacrifice, back and forth. **AHLB:** 1316-J (V) **Strong's:** 5130

208. נחה / 𐤍𐤇𐤄 / N.Hh.H **Translation:** Guide **Definition:** One who leads or directs another in his way. **AHLB:** 1307-H (V) **Strong's:** 5148

209. נחל / 𐤍𐤇𐤋 / N.Hh.L **Translation:** Inherit **Definition:** A passing down of properties, wealth or blessings to the offspring. **AHLB:** 2391 (V) **Strong's:** 5157

210. נחם / 𐤍𐤇𐤌 / N.Hh.M **Translation:** Comfort **Definition:** Consolation in time of trouble or worry; to give solace in time of difficulty or sorrow. The niphal (passive) form means "repent." **AHLB:** 2392 (V) **Strong's:** 5162

211. נטה / / N.Th.H **Translation:** Extend **Definition:** To set up camp by stretching out the cover of the tent; to extend or stretch in length. **AHLB:** 1308-H (V) **Strong's:** 5186

212. נטע / / N.Th.Ah **Translation:** Plant **Definition:** To put or set into the ground for growth; to establish plants in the sense of setting into place in the soil. **AHLB:** 2398 (V) **Strong's:** 5193

213. נטשׁ / / N.Th.Sh **Translation:** Let alone **Definition:** To be left behind by those who leave. **AHLB:** 2401 (V) **Strong's:** 5203

214. נכה / / N.K.H **Translation:** Hit **Definition:** To deliver a blow by action; to strike with the hand; to clap, kill or harm. **AHLB:** 1310-H (V) **Strong's:** 5221

215. נכר / / N.K.R **Translation:** Recognize **Definition:** To acknowledge or take notice of in some definite way. **AHLB:** 2406 (V) **Strong's:** 5234

216. נסא / / N.S.A **Translation:** Lift up **Definition:** To lift up a burden or load and carry it; to lift up camp and begin a journey; to forgive in the sense of removing the offense. **AHLB:** 1314-E (V) **Strong's:** 5375

217. נסג / / N.S.G **Translation:** Overtake **Definition:** To catch up with; to remove in the sense of taking over. **AHLB:** 2410 (V) **Strong's:** 5381

218. נסה / / N.S.H **Translation:** Test **Definition:** A critical examination, observation, or evaluation; trial. **AHLB:** 1314-H (V) **Strong's:** 5254

219. נסך / / N.S.K **Translation:** Pour **Definition:** To cause to flow in a stream; to give full expression to. **AHLB:** 2412 (V) **Strong's:** 5258

220. נסע / / N.S.Ah **Translation:** Journey **Definition:** To travel or pass from one place to another; to break camp and begin a journey. **AHLB:** 2413 (V) **Strong's:** 5265

221. נפל / / N.P.L **Translation:** Fall **Definition:** To leave an erect position suddenly and involuntarily; to descend freely by the force of gravity. **AHLB:** 2421 (V) **Strong's:** 5307

222. נצב / / N.Ts.B **Translation:** Stand up **Definition:** To be vertical in position; to stand tall and erect; to set in place. **AHLB:** 2426 (V) **Strong's:** 5324

223. נצח / / N.Ts.Hh **Translation:** Continue **Definition:** To go on or keep on, as in some course or action; to extend. **AHLB:** 2427 (V) **Strong's:** 5329

224. נצל / / N.Ts.L **Translation:** Deliver **Definition:** To set free; to take and hand over to or leave for another. **AHLB:** 2428 (V) **Strong's:** 5337

225. נצר / / N.Ts.R **Translation:** Preserve **Definition:** To watch over or guard for protection. **AHLB:** 2429 (V) **Strong's:** 5341

226. נקב / / N.Q.B **Translation:** Pierce through **Definition:** To make a hole by puncturing or penetrating; to curse in the sense of piercing through. **AHLB:** 2430 (V) **Strong's:** 5344

227. נקה / / N.Q.H **Translation:** Acquit **Definition:** To declare one innocent of a crime or oath. **AHLB:** 1318-H (V) **Strong's:** 5352

228. נקם / / N.Q.M **Translation:** Avenge **Definition:** To take vengeance for or on behalf of another; to gain satisfaction for a wrong by punishing the wrongdoer; to pursue and kill one who has murdered. **AHLB:** 2433 (V) **Strong's:** 5358

229. נשק / / N.Sh.Q **Translation:** Kiss **Definition:** To touch together as when kissing with the lips or in battle with weapons. **AHLB:** 2445 (V) **Strong's:** 5401

230. נתן / / N.T.N **Translation:** Give **Definition:** To make a present; to present a gift; to grant, allow or bestow by formal action. **AHLB:** 2451 (V) **Strong's:** 5414

231. נתץ / / N.T.Ts **Translation:** Break down **Definition:** To demolish an elevated object; to tear down. **AHLB:** 2454 (V) **Strong's:** 5422

232. נתק / / N.T.Q **Translation:** Draw **Definition:** To draw out or away as a bowstring or to draw a cord to its breaking point. **AHLB:** 2455 (V) **Strong's:** 5423

Samehh

233. סבב / 𐤎𐤁𐤁 / S.B.B **Translation:** Go around **Definition:** To circle completely around something. **AHLB:** 1324-B (V) **Strong's:** 5437

234. סגר / 𐤎𐤂𐤓 / S.G.R **Translation:** Shut **Definition:** To close or block an opening. **AHLB:** 2467 (V) **Strong's:** 5462

235. סור / 𐤎𐤅𐤓 / S.W.R **Translation:** Turn aside **Definition:** To change the location, position, station, or residence; to remove. The hiphil (causative) form means "remove." **AHLB:** 1342-J (V) **Strong's:** 5493

236. סים / 𐤎𐤉𐤌 / S.Y.M **Translation:** Place **Definition:** To put or set in a particular place, position, situation, or relation. **AHLB:** 1335-J (V) **Strong's:** 7760

237. סלח / 𐤎𐤋𐤇 / S.L.Hh **Translation:** Forgive **Definition:** To pardon; to overlook an offense and treat the offender as not guilty. **AHLB:** 2482 (V) **Strong's:** 5545

238. סמך / 𐤎𐤌𐤊 / S.M.K **Translation:** Support **Definition:** To uphold or defend; to hold up or serve as a foundation or prop for. **AHLB:** 2488 (V) **Strong's:** 5564

239. ספד / 𐤎𐤐𐤃 / S.P.D **Translation:** Lament **Definition:** To mourn aloud; wail. **AHLB:** 2495 (V) **Strong's:** 5594

240. ספר / 𐤎𐤐𐤓 / S.P.R **Translation:** Count **Definition:** To find the total number of units involved by naming the numbers in order up to and including. The piel (intensive) form means "recount." **AHLB:** 2500 (V) **Strong's:** 5608

241. סתר / 𐤎𐤕𐤓 / S.T.R **Translation:** Hide **Definition:** To put out of sight; to conceal from view; to keep secret. **AHLB:** 2516 (V) **Strong's:** 5641

Ayin

242. עבד / 𐤏𐤁𐤃 / Ah.B.D **Translation:** Serve **Definition:** To provide a service to another, as a servant or slave; to work at a profession. **AHLB:** 2518 (V) **Strong's:** 5647

243. עבר / 𐤏𐤁𐤓 / Ah.B.R **Translation:** Cross over **Definition:** To pass from one side to the other; to go across a river or through a land; to transgress in the sense of crossing over. **AHLB:** 2520 (V) **Strong's:** 5674

244. עוד / 𐤏𐤅𐤃 / Ah.W.D **Translation:** Wrap around **Definition:** To enclose; to repeat or do again what has been said or done. The hiphil (causative) form means "warn." **AHLB:** 1349-J (V) **Strong's:** 5749

245. עוף / 𐤏𐤅𐤐 / Ah.W.P **Translation:** Fly **Definition:** To move in or pass through the air with wings; to soar in the air. **AHLB:** 1362-J (V) **Strong's:** 5774

246. עור / 𐤏𐤅𐤓 / Ah.W.R **Translation:** Stir up **Definition:** To shake to awaken. **AHLB:** 1365-J (V) **Strong's:** 5782

247. עזב / 𐤏𐤆𐤁 / Ah.Z.B **Translation:** Leave **Definition:** To go away from; to neglect. **AHLB:** 2532 (V) **Strong's:** 5800

248. עזר / 𐤏𐤆𐤓 / Ah.Z.R **Translation:** Help **Definition:** To give assistance or support to. **AHLB:** 2535 (V) **Strong's:** 5826

249. עלה / 𐤏𐤋𐤄 / Ah.L.H **Translation:** Go up **Definition:** To go, come or bring higher. The hiphil (causative) form means "bring up." **AHLB:** 1357-H (V) **Strong's:** 5927

250. עלם / 𐤏𐤋𐤌 / Ah.L.M **Translation:** Be out of sight **Definition:** To be hidden or obscured from vision; to be covered or unknown. **AHLB:** 2544 (V) **Strong's:** 5956

251. עמד / 𐤏𐤌𐤃 / Ah.M.D **Translation:** Stand **Definition:** To rise, raise or set in a place. **AHLB:** 2550 (V) **Strong's:** 5975

252. ענה / 𐤏𐤍𐤄 / Ah.N.H **Translation:** Afflict **Definition:** To oppress severely so as to cause persistent suffering or anguish in the sense of making dark. **AHLB:** 1359-H (V) **Strong's:** 6031

253. ענה / 𐤏𐤍𐤄 / Ah.N.H **Translation:** Answer **Definition:** Something written or spoken in reply to a question. **AHLB:** 1520-H (V) **Strong's:** 6030

254. עצר / 𐤏𐤑𐤓 / Ah.Ts.R **Translation:** Stop **Definition:** To cause to cease; to stop from occurring in the sense of halting, shutting or restraining. **AHLB:** 2570 (V) **Strong's:** 6113

255. ערך / 𐤏𐤓𐤊 / Ah.R.K **Translation:** Arrange **Definition:** To set something in order or into a correct or suitable configuration, sequence or adjustment . **AHLB:** 2576 (V) **Strong's:** 6186

256. עשׁק / 𐤏𐤔𐤒 / Ah.Sh.Q **Translation:** Oppress **Definition:** To press into or on another through for force or deceit. **AHLB:** 2584 (V) **Strong's:** 6231

257. עשה / Ah.S.H **Translation:** Do **Definition:** To bring to pass; to bring about; to act or make. **AHLB:** 1360-H (V) **Strong's:** 6213

Pey

258. פגע / P.G.Ah **Translation:** Reach **Definition:** To touch or grasp; to get up to or as far as; to come together in meeting by chance; to give or place in the sense of a meeting. **AHLB:** 2592 (V) **Strong's:** 6293

259. פדה / P.D.H **Translation:** Ransom **Definition:** To pay the price stipulated, to retrieve what has been stolen or wrongfully taken. **AHLB:** 1372-H (V) **Strong's:** 6299

260. פוץ / P.W.Ts **Translation:** Scatter abroad **Definition:** To sow, cast or fling widely. **AHLB:** 1386-J (V) **Strong's:** 6327

261. פחד / P.Hh.D **Translation:** Shake in awe **Definition:** To physically or mentally tremble in amazement or fear. **AHLB:** 2598 (V) **Strong's:** 6342

262. פלא / P.L.A **Translation:** Perform **Definition:** To do a wondrous action that shows ones might. **AHLB:** 1380-E (V) **Strong's:** 6381

263. פלט / P.L.Th **Translation:** Deliver **Definition:** To bring out or rescue from trouble. **AHLB:** 2609 (V) **Strong's:** 6403

264. פלל / JJ⊂⊃ / P.L.L **Translation:** Plead **Definition:** To entreat or appeal earnestly; to fall to the ground to plead a cause to one in authority; prevent a judgment. **AHLB:** 1380-B (V) **Strong's:** 6419

More about the word פלל

In our modern religious culture prayer is a communication between man and Elohiym. While this definition could be applied to some passages of the Bible (such as Genesis 20:17) it is not a Hebraic definition of the Hebrew word palal. By looking at the etymology of this word we can better see the Hebraic meaning. The word palal comes from the parent root pal meaning "fall" (The root pal is most likely the root of our word fall which can etymologically be written as phal). Pal is also the root of the Hebrew word naphal also meaning "fall". The word palal literally means to "fall down to the ground in the presence of one in authority pleading a cause". This can be seen in Isaiah 45:14 where the Sabeans fall down and make supplication (this is the Hebrew word palal) to Cyrus.

265. פנה / ᛉ\⊂⊃ / P.N.H **Translation:** Turn **Definition:** To rotate or revolve; to face another direction; to turn the face; to turn directions; to turn something back or away. **AHLB:** 1382-H (V) **Strong's:** 6437

266. פעל / / P.Ah.L **Translation:** Make **Definition:** To perform a task of physical labor. **AHLB:** 2622 (V) **Strong's:** 6466

267. פקד / / P.Q.D **Translation:** Register **Definition:** To indicate or show acknowledgement of someone or something; to document or count another. **AHLB:** 2630 (V) **Strong's:** 6485

268. פרד / / P.R.D **Translation:** Divide apart **Definition:** To separate. **AHLB:** 2634 (V) **Strong's:** 6504

269. פרה / / P.R.H **Translation:** Reproduce **Definition:** To produce new individuals of the same kind; to be abundant in fruit. **AHLB:** 1388-H (V) **Strong's:** 6509

270. פרח / / P.R.Hh **Translation:** Burst out **Definition:** To be larger, fuller, or more crowded; to break out or break forth as a blooming flower or the wings of a bird. **AHLB:** 2636 (V) **Strong's:** 6524

271. פרץ / / P.R.Ts **Translation:** Break out **Definition:** To be spread out wide or widespread. **AHLB:** 2642 (V) **Strong's:** 6555

272. פרר / / P.R.R **Translation:** Break **Definition:** To throw something on the ground and break it by trampling. **AHLB:** 1388-B (V) **Strong's:** 6565

More about the word פרר

The verb parar is often translated as "break," as in "Do not break the commands of Elohiym." This word does not mean "disobey," as we often perceive it, but something much more concrete.

Each Hebrew word is a picture of action. In this case, the picture is an ox treading on the grain on the threshing floor to open up the hulls to remove the seeds. To the Ancient Hebrews, breaking the commands of Elohiym was equated with throwing it on the ground and trampling on it. A child who disobeys his parents, but is genuinely apologetic, shows honor and respect to his parents. But a child who willfully disobeys with no sign of remorse has trampled on his parents teachings and deserves punishment.

273. פרשׁ / / P.R.Sh **Translation:** Spread out **Definition:** To expand beyond a starting point; to be easily and plainly understood in the sense of being spread out to see. **AHLB:** 2644 (V) **Strong's:** 6566

274. פשׁט / / P.Sh.Th **Translation:** Peel off **Definition:** To strip off an outer layer; to spread apart; to invade in the sense of spreading out for an attack; to strip off clothing in the sense of spreading the garment for removal. **AHLB:** 2646 (V) **Strong's:** 6584

275. פשׁע / / P.Sh.Ah **Translation:** Transgress **Definition:** To pass over or go beyond a limit or boundary; to rebel. **AHLB:** 2647 (V) **Strong's:** 6586

276. פתה / / P.T.H **Translation:** Spread wide **Definition:** To lay out in a large area. The piel (intensive) form means "persuade." **AHLB:** 1390-H (V) **Strong's:** 6601

277. פתח / [pictographic script] / P.T.Hh **Translation:** Open **Definition:** To open up as opening a gate or door; to have no confining barrier. The piel (intensive) form means "engrave." **AHLB:** 2649 (V) **Strong's:** 6605

Tsade

278. צדק / [pictographic script] / Ts.D.Q **Translation:** Be correct **Definition:** To walk on the right path without losing the way. **AHLB:** 2658 (V) **Strong's:** 6663

279. צוה / [pictographic script] / Ts.W.H **Translation:** Direct **Definition:** To cause to turn, move, or point undeviatingly or to follow a straight course; give instructions or orders for a path to be taken. **AHLB:** 1397-H (V) **Strong's:** 6680

280. צור / [pictographic script] / Ts.W.R **Translation:** Smack **Definition:** To strike or push as an attack. **AHLB:** 1411-J (V) **Strong's:** 6696

281. צלח / [pictographic script] / Ts.L.Hh **Translation:** Prosper **Definition:** To succeed; to move forward in distance, position or in thriving. **AHLB:** 2662 (V) **Strong's:** 6743

282. צמח / [pictographic script] / Ts.M.Hh **Translation:** Spring up **Definition:** To grow up as a plant. **AHLB:** 2666 (V) **Strong's:** 6779

283. צעק / [pictographic script] / Ts.Ah.Q **Translation:** Cry out **Definition:** To cry or call out loudly. **AHLB:** 2679 (V) **Strong's:** 6817

284. צפה / Ts.P.H **Translation:** Keep watch **Definition:** To be on the look-out for danger or opportunity. **AHLB:** 1408-H (V) **Strong's:** 6822

285. צפה / Ts.P.H **Translation:** Overlay **Definition:** To cover with a different material, usually with gold. **AHLB:** 1408-H (V) **Strong's:** 6823

286. צפן / Ts.P.N **Translation:** Conceal **Definition:** To hide to prevent discovery. **AHLB:** 2683 (V) **Strong's:** 6845

287. צרף / Ts.R.P **Translation:** Refine **Definition:** To bring to a fine or a pure state free from impurities through smelting or testing. **AHLB:** 2692 (V) **Strong's:** 6884

288. צרר / Ts.R.R **Translation:** Press in **Definition:** To confine or restrict in a tight place. **AHLB:** 1411-B (V) **Strong's:** 6887

Quph

289. קבץ / Q.B.Ts **Translation:** Gather together **Definition:** To come or bring into a group, mass or unit. **AHLB:** 2695 (V) **Strong's:** 6908

290. קבר / Q.B.R **Translation:** Bury **Definition:** To dispose of by depositing in the ground. **AHLB:** 2696 (V) **Strong's:** 6912

291. קדם / Q.D.M **Translation:** Face toward **Definition:** To face another or meet face to face; to go before someone or something in space or time. **AHLB:** 2698 (V) **Strong's:** 6923

292. קדש / / Q.D.Sh **Translation:** Set apart **Definition:** To move or place someone or something separate from the whole for a special purpose. **AHLB:** 2700 (V) **Strong's:** 6942

293. קהל / / Q.H.L **Translation:** Round up **Definition:** To gather together a flock, herd or group of people. **AHLB:** 1426-G (V) **Strong's:** 6950

294. קוה / / Q.W.H **Translation:** Bound up **Definition:** To be confined or hedged in together; to wait or to be held back in the sense of being bound up. **AHLB:** 1419-J (V) **Strong's:** 6960

295. קום / / Q.W.M **Translation:** Rise **Definition:** To assume an upright position; to raise or rise up; to continue or establish. **AHLB:** 1427-J (V) **Strong's:** 6965

296. קטר / / Q.Th.R **Translation:** Burn incense **Definition:** To light a sacrifice or aromatic plant on fire creating smoke, often aromatic. **AHLB:** 2705 (V) **Strong's:** 6999

297. קלל / / Q.L.L **Translation:** Belittle **Definition:** To regard or portray as less impressive or important; to be light in weight; to curse or despise in the sense of making light. **AHLB:** 1426-B (V) **Strong's:** 7043

298. קנא / / Q.N.A **Translation:** Be zealous **Definition:** To be filled with eagerness and ardent interest in pursuit of something. **AHLB:** 1428-E (V) **Strong's:** 7065

299. קנה / / Q.N.H **Translation:** Purchase **Definition:** To acquire ownership or occupation through an exchange. **AHLB:** 1428-H (V) **Strong's:** 7069

300. קצף / / Q.Ts.P **Translation:** Snap **Definition:** To make a sudden closing; to break suddenly with a sharp sound; to splinter a piece of wood; to lash out in anger as a splintering. **AHLB:** 2726 (V) **Strong's:** 7107

301. קצר / / Q.Ts.R **Translation:** Sever **Definition:** To cut short or small; to harvest in the sense of severing the crop from its stalk; to be impatient in the sense of patience being severed. **AHLB:** 2727 (V) **Strong's:** 7114

302. קרא / / Q.R.A **Translation:** Call out **Definition:** To raise one's voice or speak to someone loudly and with urgency; to give, a name; to meet in the sense of being called to a meeting; to have an encounter by chance; to read in the sense of calling out words. **AHLB:** 1434-E (V) **Strong's:** 7121

303. קרב / / Q.R.B **Translation:** Come near **Definition:** To come close by or near to. The hiphil (causative) form means "bring near." **AHLB:** 2729 (V) **Strong's:** 7126

304. קרה / / Q.R.H **Translation:** Meet **Definition:** To come into the presence of; to go to meet another; to have a chance encounter. **AHLB:** 1434-H (V) **Strong's:** 7125

305. קרע / / Q.R.Ah **Translation:** Tear **Definition:** To rip into pieces. **AHLB:** 2734 (V) **Strong's:** 7167

306. קשׁב / / Q.Sh.B **Translation:** Heed **Definition:** To hear and pay attention. **AHLB:** 2737 (V) **Strong's:** 7181

307. קשה / 𐤒𐤔𐤄 / Q.Sh.H **Translation:** Be hard **Definition:** To be difficult; not easily penetrated; not easily yielding to pressure. **AHLB:** 1435-H (V) **Strong's:** 7185

308. קשר / 𐤒𐤔𐤓 / Q.Sh.R **Translation:** Tie **Definition:** To fasten, attach, or close by means of a string or cord; to tie around; to conspire in the sense of tying up. **AHLB:** 2740 (V) **Strong's:** 7194

Resh

309. ראה / 𐤓𐤀𐤄 / R.A.H **Translation:** See **Definition:** To take notice; to perceive something or someone; to see visions. The niphal (passive) form means "appear" and the hiphil (causative) form means "show." **AHLB:** 1438-H (V) **Strong's:** 7200

310. רבה / 𐤓𐤁𐤄 / R.B.H **Translation:** Increase **Definition:** To become progressively greater; to multiply by the production of young; to be abundant of number, strength or authority. **AHLB:** 1439-H (V) **Strong's:** 7235

311. רבץ / 𐤓𐤁𐤑 / R.B.Ts **Translation:** Stretch out **Definition:** To lie or stretch out as to rest; to crouch down to hide for an ambush. **AHLB:** 2745 (V) **Strong's:** 7257

312. רגז / 𐤓𐤂𐤆 / R.G.Z **Translation:** Shake **Definition:** To tremble in fear or anger. **AHLB:** 2748 (V) **Strong's:** 7264

313. רגל / 𐤓𐤂𐤋 / R.G.L **Translation:** Tread about **Definition:** To be on foot walking through a foreign land, usually in the sense of spying; to trample another with the tongue. **AHLB:** 2749 (V) **Strong's:** 7270

314. רדה / 𐤓𐤃𐤄 / R.D.H **Translation:** Rule **Definition:** To exert control, direction, or influence over, especially by curbing or restraining; to spread out through a land through authority or by walking among the subjects. **AHLB:** 1441-H (V) **Strong's:** 7287

315. רדף / 𐤓𐤃𐤐 / R.D.P **Translation:** Pursue **Definition:** To follow in order to overtake, capture, kill, or defeat; to pursue in chase or persecution. **AHLB:** 2755 (V) **Strong's:** 7291

316. רום / 𐤓𐤅𐤌 / R.W.M **Translation:** Raise **Definition:** To lift something up. **AHLB:** 1450-J (V) **Strong's:** 7311

317. רוע / 𐤓𐤅𐤏 / R.W.Ah **Translation:** Shout **Definition:** To shout an alarm of war or for great rejoicing. **AHLB:** 1460-J (V) **Strong's:** 7321

318. רוץ / 𐤓𐤅𐤑 / R.W.Ts **Translation:** Run **Definition:** To go faster than a walk. **AHLB:** 1455-J (V) **Strong's:** 7323

319. רחב / 𐤓𐤇𐤁 / R.Hh.B **Translation:** Widen **Definition:** To increase the size of an area wide; large; roomy. **AHLB:** 2759 (V) **Strong's:** 7337

320. רחם / 𐤓𐤇𐤌 / R.Hh.M **Translation:** Have compassion **Definition:** To have a feeling of deep sympathy and sorrow for another who is stricken by misfortune, accompanied by a strong desire to alleviate the suffering. **AHLB:** 2762 (V) **Strong's:** 7355

321. רחץ / / R.Hh.Ts **Translation:** Bathe **Definition:** To cleanse by being immersed in, or washing with, water. **AHLB:** 2764 (V) **Strong's:** 7364

322. רחק / / R.Hh.Q **Translation:** Be far **Definition:** To be distant, a long way off. **AHLB:** 2765 (V) **Strong's:** 7368

323. ריב / / R.Y.B **Translation:** Dispute **Definition:** To engage in argument; to dispute or chide another in harassment or trial. **AHLB:** 1439-M (V) **Strong's:** 7378

324. רכב / / R.K.B **Translation:** Vehicle **Definition:** A wheeled transport such as a wagon or chariot used for transportation. Also, the top millstone as a wheel that rides on top of the lower millstone. **AHLB:** 2769 (V) **Strong's:** 7392

325. רנן / / R.N.N **Translation:** Shout aloud **Definition:** To cry out loudly in triumph or joy. **AHLB:** 1451-B (V) **Strong's:** 7442

326. רעה / / R.Ah.H **Translation:** Feed **Definition:** To give food to; to provide feed or pasture to the flock. Commonly used in the participle form meaning a feeder or shepherd. **AHLB:** 1453-H (V) **Strong's:** 7462

327. רעע / / R.Ah.Ah **Translation:** Be dysfunctional **Definition:** Impaired or abnormal filling of purpose; to act wrongly by injuring or doing an evil action. **AHLB:** 1460-B (V) **Strong's:** 7489

328. רעש / / R.Ah.Sh **Translation:** Quake **Definition:** To violently shake. **AHLB:** 2784 (V) **Strong's:** 7493

329. רפא / 𐤓𐤐𐤀 / R.P.A **Translation:** Heal **Definition:** To restore to health or wholeness. **AHLB:** 1454-E (V) **Strong's:** 7495

330. רפה / 𐤓𐤐𐤄 / R.P.H **Translation:** Sink down **Definition:** To drop down; to be slack or idle due to weakness, illness or laziness. The niphal (passive) form means "lazy." **AHLB:** 1454-H (V) **Strong's:** 7503

331. רצה / 𐤓𐤑𐤄 / R.Ts.H **Translation:** Accept **Definition:** To receive from the messenger what is given as a message. **AHLB:** 1455-H (V) **Strong's:** 7521

332. רצח / 𐤓𐤑𐤇 / R.Ts.Hh **Translation:** Murder **Definition:** A killing committed with malice aforethought, characterized by deliberation or premeditation. **AHLB:** 2790 (V) **Strong's:** 7523

333. רשׁע / 𐤓𐤔𐤏 / R.Sh.Ah **Translation:** Depart **Definition:** To go astray from the correct path and become lost; to act against a law or teaching as one who has gone astray. The hiphil (causative) form means "convict." **AHLB:** 2799 (V) **Strong's:** 7561

Shin

334. שׁאל / 𐤔𐤀𐤋 / Sh.A.L **Translation:** Enquire **Definition:** To ask about; to search into; to seek to understand what is not known. The hiphil (causative) form means "grant." **AHLB:** 1472-D (V) **Strong's:** 7592

335. שאר / / Sh.A.R **Translation:** Remain **Definition:** To continue unchanged; to stay behind. **AHLB:** 1480-D (V) **Strong's:** 7604

336. שבה / / Sh.B.H **Translation:** Capture **Definition:** The act of catching, winning, or gaining control by force, stratagem, or guile; to take one away from his homeland as an involuntary prisoner. **AHLB:** 1462-H (V) **Strong's:** 7617

337. שבע / / Sh.B.Ah **Translation:** Swear **Definition:** To completely submit to a promise or oath with words and spoken seven times. **AHLB:** 2808 (V) **Strong's:** 7650

338. שבר / / Sh.B.R **Translation:** Crack **Definition:** To break open, apart or into pieces. The piel (intensive) form means "shatter." **AHLB:** 2811 (V) **Strong's:** 7665

339. שבת / / Sh.B.T **Translation:** Cease **Definition:** To come to an end; to die out; to stop an activity for the purpose of rest or celebration. **AHLB:** 2812 (V) **Strong's:** 7673

340. שדד / / Sh.D.D **Translation:** Spoil **Definition:** To dry up and shrivel and be of no use. **AHLB:** 1464-B (V) **Strong's:** 7703

341. שוב / / Sh.W.B **Translation:** Turn back **Definition:** To return to a previous place or state. **AHLB:** 1462-J (V) **Strong's:** 7725

342. שחה / / Sh.Hh.H **Translation:** Bend down **Definition:** To pay homage to another one by bowing low or getting on the knees with the face to the ground. **AHLB:** 1468-H (V) **Strong's:** 7812

More about the word שחה

In our modern western culture worship is an action directed toward Elohiym and Elohiym alone. But this is not the case in the Hebrew Bible. The word shahhah is a common Hebrew verb meaning to prostrate oneself before another in respect, or simply, obeisance. We see Moses doing this to his father-in-law in Exodus 18:7. From a Hebraic perspective obeisance is the act of getting down on ones knees and placing the face down on the ground before another worthy of respect.

343. שחט / ⊗ⵎш / Sh.Hh.Th **Translation:** Slay **Definition:** To strike, beat or kill. **AHLB:** 2823 (V) **Strong's:** 7819

344. שחת / +ⵎш / Sh.Hh.T **Translation:** Damage **Definition:** To bring to ruin by destruction; to destroy through disfigurement or corruption. **AHLB:** 2830 (V) **Strong's:** 7843

345. שטף / ⊂⊃⊗ш / Sh.Th.P **Translation:** Flush **Definition:** To flow over with copious amounts of water. **AHLB:** 2832 (V) **Strong's:** 7857

346. שיר / ⍝⅃ш / Sh.Y.R **Translation:** Sing **Definition:** To express one's voice in a melody or to music. **AHLB:** 1480-M (V) **Strong's:** 7891

347. שית / +⅃ш / Sh.Y.T **Translation:** Set down **Definition:** To cause to sit down; to lay down. **AHLB:** 1482-M (V) **Strong's:** 7896

348. שכב / / Sh.K.B **Translation:** Lay down **Definition:** To give up; to lie down for copulation, rest or sleep. **AHLB:** 2834 (V) **Strong's:** 7901

349. שכח / / Sh.K.Hh **Translation:** Forget **Definition:** To lose remembrance of; to cease remembering or noticing. **AHLB:** 2835 (V) **Strong's:** 7911

350. שכם / / Sh.K.M **Translation:** Depart early **Definition:** Literally, to put a load on the shoulder to go away or leave early. **AHLB:** 2837 (V) **Strong's:** 7925

351. שכן / / Sh.K.N **Translation:** Dwell **Definition:** To remain for a time; to live as a resident; to stay or sit in one location for an indeterminate duration. **AHLB:** 2838 (V) **Strong's:** 7931

352. שלח / / Sh.L.Hh **Translation:** Send **Definition:** To cause to go; to direct, order, or request to go. **AHLB:** 2842 (V) **Strong's:** 7971

353. שלך / / Sh.L.K **Translation:** Throw out **Definition:** To remove from a place, usually in a sudden or unexpected manner; to cast out, down or away. **AHLB:** 2844 (V) **Strong's:** 7993

354. שלם / / Sh.L.M **Translation:** Make restitution **Definition:** To restore or make right through action, payment or restoration to a rightful owner. **AHLB:** 2845 (V) **Strong's:** 7999

355. שמד / / Sh.M.D **Translation:** Destroy **Definition:** To bring to ruin a structure, existence, or condition. **AHLB:** 2848 (V) **Strong's:** 8045

356. שמם / / Sh.M.M **Translation:** Desolate **Definition:** To be devoid of inhabitants or visitors. **AHLB:** 1473-B (V) **Strong's:** 8074

357. שמע / / Sh.M.Ah **Translation:** Hear **Definition:** To perceive or apprehend by the ear; to listen to with attention. **AHLB:** 2851 (V) **Strong's:** 8085

358. שמר / / Sh.M.R **Translation:** Safeguard **Definition:** The act or the duty of protecting or defending; to watch over or guard in the sense of preserving or protecting. **AHLB:** 2853 (V) **Strong's:** 8104

More about the word שמר

The image painted by the Hebrew word shamar is a sheepfold. When a shepherd was out in the wilderness with his flock, he would gather thorn bushes to erect a corral to place his flock in at night. The thorns would deter predators and thereby protect and guard the sheep from harm. The word shamiyr, derived from this root means a thorn. The word shamar means to guard and protect and can be seen in the Aaronic blessing, May Yahweh respect you and guard you. One keeps the commands of Elohiym by guarding and protecting them.

359. שפט / / Sh.P.Th **Translation:** Decide **Definition:** To make a determination in a dispute or wrong doing. **AHLB:** 2864 (V) **Strong's:** 8199

360. שפך / / Sh.P.K **Translation:** Pour out **Definition:** To let flow a liquid, often the blood of an animal in sacrifice or a man. **AHLB:** 2865 (V) **Strong's:** 8210

361. שפל / / Sh.P.L **Translation:** Low **Definition:** To be small in position or stature. **AHLB:** 2866 (V) **Strong's:** 8213

362. שקה / / Sh.Q.H **Translation:** Drink **Definition:** To swallow liquid, whether of man or of the land. **AHLB:** 1479-H (V) **Strong's:** 8248

363. שקט / / Sh.Q.Th **Translation:** Tranquil **Definition:** To be quiet and at rest. **AHLB:** 2873 (V) **Strong's:** 8252

364. שרת / / Sh.R.T **Translation:** Minister **Definition:** To give aid or service; to be in service to another. **AHLB:** 2884 (V) **Strong's:** 8334

365. שתה / / Sh.T.H **Translation:** Gulp **Definition:** To drink plentifully; to swallow hurriedly or greedily or in one swallow. **AHLB:** 1482-H (V) **Strong's:** 8354

366. שבע / / S.B.Ah **Translation:** Be satisfied **Definition:** To be filled full or to overflowing; to have a complete amount. **AHLB:** 2461 (V) **Strong's:** 7646

367. שחק / / S.Hh.Q **Translation:** Laugh **Definition:** To laugh in play, sport or scorn. **AHLB:** 2472 (V) **Strong's:** 7832

368. שכל / / S.K.L **Translation:** Calculate **Definition:** To determine by mathematical deduction or practical judgment; to comprehend and carefully consider a path or course of action. **AHLB:** 2477 (V) **Strong's:** 7919

369. שׂמח / 𐤔𐤌𐤇 / S.M.Hh **Translation:** Rejoice **Definition:** To be happy, glad. **AHLB:** 2487 (V) **Strong's:** 8055

370. שׂנא / 𐤔𐤍𐤀 / S.N.A **Translation:** Hate **Definition:** Intense hostility and aversion, usually deriving from fear, anger, or sense of injury; extreme dislike or antipathy. **AHLB:** 1336-E (V) **Strong's:** 8130

371. שׂרף / 𐤔𐤓𐤐 / S.R.P **Translation:** Cremate **Definition:** To reduce a dead body, or other object, to ashes by burning. **AHLB:** 2512 (V) **Strong's:** 8313

372. שׂוּשׂ / 𐤔𐤅𐤔 / S.W.S **Translation:** Skip **Definition:** To move with quick steps in joy. **AHLB:** 1337-J (V) **Strong's:** 7797

373. שׁטר / 𐤔𐤈𐤓 / Sh.Th.R **Translation:** Dominate **Definition:** To govern or prevail over as a magistrate; to be in ultimate control; to establish order. **AHLB:** 2833 (V) **Strong's:** 7860

374. שׁכל / 𐤔𐤊𐤋 / Sh.K.L **Translation:** Be childless **Definition:** To be without children through miscarriage, barrenness or loss of children. **AHLB:** 2836 (V) **Strong's:** 7921

Tav

375. תלה / 𐤕𐤋𐤄 / T.L.H **Translation:** Hang **Definition:** To suspend with no support from below. **AHLB:** 1495-H (V) **Strong's:** 8518

376. תמם / 𐤕𐤌𐤌 / T.M.M **Translation:** Be whole **Definition:** To be free of wound or injury, defect or impairment, disease or deformity; physically and mentally sound. **AHLB:** 1496-B (V) **Strong's:** 8552

377. תעה / 𐤕𐤏𐤄 / T.Ah.H **Translation:** Wander **Definition:** To go astray due to deception or influence. **AHLB:** 1499-H (V) **Strong's:** 8582

378. תפש / 𐤕𐤐𐤔 / T.P.S **Translation:** Seize hold **Definition:** To take hold of something by force. **AHLB:** 2899 (V) **Strong's:** 8610

379. תקע / 𐤕𐤒𐤏 / T.Q.Ah **Translation:** Thrust **Definition:** To push or drive with force a pole into the ground, such as when setting up the tent; to blow the trumpet in the sense of throwing out the sound. **AHLB:** 2902 (V) **Strong's:** 8628

Dictionary ~ Nouns

Aleph

380. אָב / [pictographic] / av **Translation:** Father **Definition:** A man who has begotten a child. The provider and support to the household. The ancestor of a family line. The patron of a profession or art. **AHLB:** 1002-A (N) **Strong's:** 1

More about the word אָב

In the original pictographic script, the first letter is a picture of an ox. As the ox is strong, the letter also has the meaning of strong. The second letter is the picture of the tent or house where the family resides. When combined, these letters form the meaning "the strength of the house."

381. אֶבְיוֹן / [pictographic] / ev-yon **Translation:** Needy **Definition:** In a condition of need or want. **AHLB:** 1033-C (j) **Strong's:** 34

382. אֶבֶן / [pictographic] / e-ven **Translation:** Stone **Definition:** A piece of rock, often in the context of building material. **AHLB:** 1037-C (N) **Strong's:** 68

383. אָדוֹן / / a-don **Translation:** Lord **Definition:** The ruler as the foundation to the community. **AHLB:** 1083-C (c) **Strong's:** 113

384. אֲדוֹנָי / / a-do-nai **Translation:** My lord **Definition:** A name often used for YHWH. **AHLB:** 1083-C (N) **Strong's:** 136

385. אַדִּיר / / a-dir **Translation:** Eminent **Definition:** What exerts power and status. Someone or something that is wide in authority or majesty. **AHLB:** 1089-C (b) **Strong's:** 117

386. אָדָם / / a-dam **Translation:** Human **Definition:** Of, relating to, or characteristic of man. The first man. All of mankind as the descendants of the first man. **AHLB:** 1082-C (N) **Strong's:** 120

387. אֲדָמָה / / a-da-mah **Translation:** Ground **Definition:** The surface of the earth. From its reddish color. **AHLB:** 1082-C (N1) **Strong's:** 127

388. אֶדֶן / / e-den **Translation:** Footing **Definition:** Ground or basis for a firm foundation. That which sustains a stable position. **AHLB:** 1083-C (N) **Strong's:** 134

389. אַהֲבָה / / a-ha-vah **Translation:** Affection **Definition:** A moderate feeling or emotion. A tender attachment or fondness. **AHLB:** 1094-C (N) **Strong's:** 160

390. אֹהֶל / / o-hel **Translation:** Tent **Definition:** The black, goat hair dwelling of the nomad. **AHLB:** 1104-C (g) **Strong's:** 168

391. אֱוִיל / 𐤀𐤅𐤉𐤋 / e-vil **Translation:** Foolish **Definition:** One who acts without consideration or regard for a desirable outcome. **AHLB:** 1254-J (b) **Strong's:** 191

392. אוּלָם / 𐤀𐤅𐤋𐤌 / u-lam **Translation:** Porch **Definition:** An exterior appendage to a building, forming a covered approach or vestibule to a doorway. **AHLB:** 1266-C (o) **Strong's:** 197

393. אָוֶן / 𐤀𐤅𐤍 / a-ven **Translation:** Vanity **Definition:** Action or thought that is vain or for an improper purpose. **AHLB:** 1014-J (N) **Strong's:** 205

394. אוֹפָן / 𐤀𐤅𐤐𐤍 / o-phen **Translation:** Wheel **Definition:** A circular frame or disk arranged to revolve on an axis, as on a wagon or chariot. **AHLB:** 1382-C (g) **Strong's:** 212

395. אוֹצָר / 𐤀𐤅𐤑𐤓 / o-tsar **Translation:** Storehouse **Definition:** A place where grain or other items of subsistence are held and protected. **AHLB:** 1411-C (g) **Strong's:** 214

396. אוֹר / 𐤀𐤅𐤓 / or **Translation:** Light **Definition:** The illumination from the sun, moon, stars, fire, candle or other source. **AHLB:** 1020-J (N) **Strong's:** 216

397. אוֹת / 𐤀𐤅𐤕 / ot **Translation:** Sign **Definition:** The motion, gesture, or mark representing an agreement between two parties. A wondrous or miraculous sign. **AHLB:** 1022-J (N) **Strong's:** 226

398. אֹזֶן / 𐤀𐤅𐤆𐤍 / o-zen **Translation:** Ear **Definition:** The organ of hearing; so named from its broad shape. **AHLB:** 1152-C (g) **Strong's:** 241

399. אָח / 𐤀𐤇 / ahh **Translation:** Brother **Definition:** A male who has the same parents as another or shares one parent with another. One who stands between the enemy and the family, a protector. **AHLB:** 1008-A (N) **Strong's:** 251

More about the word אָח

The first letter is the picture of an ox. As the ox is strong, the letter also has the meaning of strong. The second letter is the picture of a tent wall. The wall is a wall of protection which protects what is inside from what is outside. When combined these letters form the word meaning "the strong wall" and represents the "brother" as the protector of the family.

400. אֶחָד / 𐤀𐤇𐤃 / e-hhad **Translation:** Unit **Definition:** A unit within the whole, a unified group. A single quantity. **AHLB:** 1165-C (N) **Strong's:** 259

More about the word אֶחָד

The word ehhad (noun) comes from the verbal root ahhad meaning "to unite." Ehhad is best translated with the word "unit," something that is part of the whole, a unit within a community. In the Hebrew mind everything is, or should be, a part of a unity. There is not one tree but a tree composed of units within the unity-roots, trunk, branches and leaves. A tree is also in unity with the other trees-the forest. A son is a unit within the brotherhood and the family.

401. אָחוֹר / 𐤀𐤇𐤅𐤓 / a-hhor **Translation:** Back **Definition:** The part of the body that is behind. To be in the rear of or behind something. **AHLB:** 1181-C (c) **Strong's:** 268

402. אָחוֹת / 𐤀𐤇𐤅𐤕 / a-hhot **Translation:** Sister **Definition:** A female person having the same parents or parent as another person. **AHLB:** 1008-A (N3) **Strong's:** 269

403. אֲחֻזָּה / 𐤀𐤇𐤅𐤆𐤄 / a-hhu-zah **Translation:** Holdings **Definition:** Property that is held or owned. **AHLB:** 1168-C (N1) **Strong's:** 272

404. אַחֵר / 𐤀𐤇𐤓 / a-hheyr **Translation:** Other **Definition:** One that remains of two or more. A time, person or thing that follows after. **AHLB:** 1181-C (N) **Strong's:** 312

405. אַחַר / 𐤀𐤇𐤓𐤉 / a-hhar **Translation:** After **Definition:** A time to come beyond another event. **AHLB:** 1181-C (N) **Strong's:** 310

406. אַחֲרוֹן / 𐤀𐤇𐤓𐤅𐤍 / a-hha-ron **Translation:** Last **Definition:** In, to or toward the back . To be in back of, at the rear or following after something. **AHLB:** 1181-C (j) **Strong's:** 314

407. אַחֲרִית / 𐤀𐤇𐤓𐤉𐤕 / a-hha-rit **Translation:** End **Definition:** A final point that marks the extent of something. The latter time as coming after everything else. **AHLB:** 1181-C (N4) **Strong's:** 319

408. אִי / 𐤀𐤍𐤉 / i **Translation:** Island **Definition:** A tract of land surrounded by water. **AHLB:** 1014-A (f) **Strong's:** 339

409. אַיִל / / a-yil **Translation:** Buck **Definition:** The large males of a flock of sheep or heard of deer. By extension, anything of strength including a chief, pillar (as the strong support of a building), or oak tree (one of the strongest of the woods). **AHLB:** 1012-M (N) **Strong's:** 352

410. אֵיפָה / / ey-phah **Translation:** Eyphah **Definition:** A dry standard of measure equal to 3 se'ahs or 10 omers. The same as the liquid measure bath which is about 9 imperial gallons or 40 liters. **AHLB:** 1017-M (N1) **Strong's:** 374

411. אִישׁ / / ish **Translation:** Man **Definition:** An adult male human. As mortal. Also, used to mean "each" in the sense of an individual. **AHLB:** 2003 (b) **Strong's:** 376

412. אֹכֶל / / o-khel **Translation:** Foodstuff **Definition:** A substance that may be eaten for giving sustenance and making one whole. **AHLB:** 1242-C (g) **Strong's:** 400

413. אֵל / / eyl **Translation:** Mighty one **Definition:** One who holds authority over others, such as a judge, chief or god. In the sense of being yoked to one another. **AHLB:** 1012-A (N) **Strong's:** 410

More about the word אֵל

When reading the Bible it is better to have an Ancient Hebrew perception of Elohiym rather than our modern western view. The word el was originally written with two pictographic letters, one being an ox head and the other a shepherd staff. The ox represented strength and the staff of the shepherd represented authority. First, the Ancient Hebrews saw Elohiym as the strong one of authority. The shepherd staff was also understood as a staff on the shoulders, a yoke. Secondly, the Ancient Hebrews saw Elohiym as the ox in the yoke. When plowing a field two oxen were placed in a yoke, one was the older more experienced one, and the other was the younger and less experienced. The younger would then learn from the older. The Hebrews saw Elohiym as the older experienced ox and they as the younger that learns from him.

414. אָלָה / / a-lah **Translation:** Oath **Definition:** Something corroborated by a vow. A binding agreement, including the curse for violating the oath. **AHLB:** 1012-A (N1) **Strong's:** 423

415. אֱלֹהִים / / e-lo-him **Translation:** Powers **Definition:** May be a plural noun meaning great strength, or the name - elohiym. **AHLB:** 1012-H (c) **Strong's:** 430

More about the word אֱלֹהִים

The plural form of elo'ah, meaning power, is elohiym and is often translated as Elohiym. While English plurals only identify quantity, as in more than one, the Hebrew plural can identify quantity as well as quality. Something that is of great size or stature can be written in the plural form. Elohiym is the one of great strength and authority.

416. אֱלוֹהַּ / / e-lo-ah **Translation:** Power **Definition:** Possession of control, authority, or influence over others; physical might. The power or might of one who rules or teaches. One who yokes with another. Often applies to rulers or a god. **AHLB:** 1012-H (c) **Strong's:** 433

417. אַלּוּף / / a-luph **Translation:** Chief **Definition:** Accorded highest rank or office; of greatest importance, significance, or influence. One who is yoked to another to lead and teach. **AHLB:** 2001 (d) **Strong's:** 441

418. אַלְמָנָה / / al-ma-nah **Translation:** Widow **Definition:** A woman who has lost her husband by death. As bound in grief. **AHLB:** 1266-C (m1) **Strong's:** 490

419. אֵם / / eym **Translation:** Mother **Definition:** A female parent. Maternal tenderness or affection. One who fulfills the role of a mother. **AHLB:** 1013-A (N) **Strong's:** 517

More about the word אֵם

In the original pictographic script, the first letter is a picture of an ox. As the ox is strong, the letter also has the meaning of strong. The second letter represents water. The two letters give us the meaning of "strong water." The Hebrews made glue by boiling animal skins in water. As the skin broke down, a sticky thick liquid formed at the surface of the water. This thick liquid was removed and used as a binding agent-"strong water". This is the Hebrew word meaning "mother", the one who "binds" the family together.

420. אַמָּה / am-mah **Translation:** Forearm **Definition:** A linear standard of measure equal to the length of the forearm. **AHLB:** 1013-A (N1) **Strong's:** 520

421. אָמָה / a-mah **Translation:** Bondwoman **Definition:** A female slave. One who is bound to another. **AHLB:** 1013-A (N1) **Strong's:** 519

422. אֱמוּנָה / e-mu-nah **Translation:** Firmness **Definition:** Securely fixed in place. **AHLB:** 1290-C (d1) **Strong's:** 530

More about the word אֱמוּנָה

The Hebrew root aman means firm, something that is supported or secure. This word is used in Isaiah 22:23 for a nail that is fastened to a "secure" place. Derived from this root is the word emun, meaning craftsman. A craftsman is one who is firm and secure in his talent. The feminine form of emun is the word emunah meaning firmness, something or someone that is firm in their actions. When the Hebrew word emunah is translated as "faith," as it often is, misconceptions of its meaning occur. Faith is usually perceived as a knowing while the Hebrew emunah is a firm action. To have faith in Elohiym is not knowing that Elohiym exists or knowing that he will act, rather it is that the one with emunah will act with firmness toward Elohiym's will.

423. אָמֵן / / a-meyn **Translation:** So be it **Definition:** An affirmation of firmness and support. **AHLB:** 1290-C (N) **Strong's:** 543

424. אֵמֶר / / ey-mer **Translation:** Statement **Definition:** A single declaration or remark. **AHLB:** 1288-C (N) **Strong's:** 561

425. אִמְרָה / / im-rah **Translation:** Speech **Definition:** The chain of words when speaking. **AHLB:** 1288-C (N1) **Strong's:** 565

426. אֱמֶת / / e-met **Translation:** Truth **Definition:** The state of being the case. Fact. What is firm. Accurately so. **AHLB:** 1290-C (N2) **Strong's:** 571

More about the word אֱמֶת

The root of this word is aman, a word often translated as "believe," but more literally means "support," as we see in Isaiah 22:23 where it says "I will drive him like a peg in a place of support..." A belief in Elohiym is not a mental exercise of knowing that Elohiym exists but rather our responsibility to show him our support. The word "emet" has the similar meaning of firmness, something that is firmly set in place. Psalms 119:142 says, "the "Torah" (the teachings of Elohiym) is "emet" (set firmly in place).

427. אֱנוֹשׁ / 𐤀𐤍𐤅𐤔 / e-nosh **Translation:** Person **Definition:** An individual, a man. **AHLB:** 2003 (c) **Strong's:** 582

428. אַף / 𐤀𐤐 / aph **Translation:** Nose **Definition:** The organ bearing the nostrils on the anterior of the face. The nostrils when used in the plural form. Also meaning anger from the flaring of the nostrils when angry. **AHLB:** 1017-A (N) **Strong's:** 639

More about the word אַף

This word is a good example that demonstrates the concrete nature of the Hebrew Language. This is the Hebrew word for a "nose," or "nostrils" when written in the plural form (נפים - naphiym), but can also mean "anger." When one becomes very angry, the nostrils start flaring. A literal interpretation of 1 Samuel 20:34 is, "And Jonathon rose from the table with a burning nose," where the phrase "burning nose" means a "fierce anger."

429. אֵפוֹד / 𐤀𐤐𐤅𐤃 / ey-phod **Translation:** Ephod **Definition:** An apron-like vestment having two shoulder straps and ornamental attachments for securing the breastplate, worn with a waistband by the high priest. **AHLB:** 1372-C (c) **Strong's:** 646

430. אֶפֶס / 𐤀𐤐𐤎 / e-phes **Translation:** End **Definition:** The concluding part of an area or extremity. Also used for the conclusion of a thought; finally, however, but. **AHLB:** 1383-C (N) **Strong's:** 657

431. אֶצְבַּע / / ets-ba **Translation:** Finger **Definition:** The extension of the hand. Can be used to point. **AHLB:** 2655 (n) **Strong's:** 676

432. אֵצֶל / / ey-tsel **Translation:** Beside **Definition:** Being next to something. **AHLB:** 1403-C (N) **Strong's:** 681

433. אַרְגָּמָן / / ar-ga-man **Translation:** Purple **Definition:** A reddish-blue color used to dye yarn and used in weaving. **AHLB:** 1440-C (pm) **Strong's:** 713

434. אֲרוֹן / / a-ron **Translation:** Box **Definition:** A rigid rectangular receptacle often with a cover. Any box-shaped object. **AHLB:** 1020-H (j) **Strong's:** 727

435. אֶרֶז / / e-rez **Translation:** Cedar **Definition:** A coniferous tree from the Cyprus family having wide, spreading branches. The wood or tree or something made it. **AHLB:** 1444-C (N) **Strong's:** 730

436. אֹרַח / / o-rahh **Translation:** Path **Definition:** The road or route one travels. **AHLB:** 1445-C (g) **Strong's:** 734

437. אֲרִי / / a-ri **Translation:** Lion **Definition:** A large carnivorous chiefly nocturnal cat. A feared animal. **AHLB:** 1442-H (b) **Strong's:** 738

438. אֹרֶךְ / / o-rek **Translation:** Length **Definition:** A measured distance or dimension. **AHLB:** 1448-C (g) **Strong's:** 753

439. אַרְמוֹן / / ar-mon **Translation:** Citadel **Definition:** A large palace or fortress usually constructed in a high place. **AHLB:** 1450-C (j) **Strong's:** 759

440. אֶרֶץ / / e-rets **Translation:** Land **Definition:** The solid part of the earth's surface. The whole of the earth or a region. **AHLB:** 1455-C (N) **Strong's:** 776

441. אֵשׁ / / eysh **Translation:** Fire **Definition:** The phenomenon of combustion manifested by heat, light and flame. **AHLB:** 1021-A (N) **Strong's:** 784

442. אִשֶּׁה / / i-sheh **Translation:** Fire offering **Definition:** A sacrifice that is placed in a fire as an offering. **AHLB:** 1021-H (e) **Strong's:** 801

443. אִשָּׁה / / i-shah **Translation:** Woman **Definition:** An adult female person. As mortal. **AHLB:** 2003 (b1) **Strong's:** 802

444. אָשָׁם / / a-sham **Translation:** Guilt **Definition:** The fact of having committed a breach of conduct especially violating law and involving a penalty; the state of one who has committed an offense, especially consciously. **AHLB:** 1473-C (N) **Strong's:** 817

445. אֶשֶׁר / / a-sheyr **Translation:** Happy **Definition:** A feeling of joy or satisfaction. **AHLB:** 1480-C (N) **Strong's:** 835

446. אֲשֵׁרָה / / a-shey-rah **Translation:** Grove **Definition:** An area of planted trees. Trees planted in a straight line. **AHLB:** 1480-C (N) **Strong's:** 842

447. אָתוֹן / 𐤀𐤕𐤅𐤍 / a-ton **Translation:** She-donkey **Definition:** A female ass. **AHLB:** 1497-C (c) **Strong's:** 860

Beyt

448. בְּאֵר / 𐤁𐤀𐤓 / b-eyr **Translation:** Well **Definition:** A dug-out hole, usually a well or cistern. **AHLB:** 1250-D (N) **Strong's:** 875

449. בֶּגֶד / 𐤁𐤂𐤃 / be-ged **Translation:** Garment **Definition:** An article of clothing for covering. **AHLB:** 2004 (N) **Strong's:** 899

450. בַּד / 𐤁𐤃 / bad **Translation:** Stick **Definition:** A branch or staff as separated from the tree. Linen cloth, from its stiff and divided fibers. Often used in the idiom "to his/her own stick" meaning alone or self. **AHLB:** 1027-A (N) **Strong's:** 905

451. בְּהֵמָה / 𐤁𐤄𐤌𐤄 / b-hey-mah **Translation:** Beast **Definition:** An animal as distinguished from man or a plant. A tall or large creature. **AHLB:** 1036-G (N1) **Strong's:** 929

452. בּוֹר / 𐤁𐤅𐤓 / bor **Translation:** Cistern **Definition:** An artificial reservoir for storing water. A hole or well as dug out. **AHLB:** 1250-J (N) **Strong's:** 953

453. בַּז / 𐤁𐤆 / baz **Translation:** Spoils **Definition:** Something that is seized by violence and robbery; prey; booty. **AHLB:** 1030-A (N) **Strong's:** 957

454. בָּחוּר / [Ancient Hebrew] / ba-hhur **Translation:** Youth **Definition:** A young person as one chosen for an activity. **AHLB:** 2012 (d) **Strong's:** 970

455. בֶּטַח / [Ancient Hebrew] / be-tahh **Translation:** Safely **Definition:** A state or place of safety. **AHLB:** 2013 (N) **Strong's:** 983

456. בֶּטֶן / [Ancient Hebrew] / be-ten **Translation:** Womb **Definition:** An organ where something is generated or grows before birth. **AHLB:** 2015 (N) **Strong's:** 990

457. בֵּין / [Ancient Hebrew] / beyn **Translation:** Between **Definition:** In the time, space or interval that separates. **AHLB:** 1037-M (N) **Strong's:** 996

458. בִּינָה / [Ancient Hebrew] / bi-nah **Translation:** Understanding **Definition:** A comprehension of the construction of a structure or thought. **AHLB:** 1037-M (N1) **Strong's:** 998

459. בַּיִת / [Ancient Hebrew] / ba-yit **Translation:** House **Definition:** The structure or the family, as a household that resides within the house. A housing. Within. **AHLB:** 1045-M (N) **Strong's:** 1004

460. בְּכוֹר / [Ancient Hebrew] / b-khor **Translation:** Firstborn **Definition:** The firstborn offspring, usually a son, of a man or animal. The prominent one. **AHLB:** 2016 (c) **Strong's:** 1060

More about the word בְּכוֹר

The firstborn of the father receives a double portion of the inheritance as well as being the leader of his brothers. However, if a son other than the firstborn receives this inheritance, he is called the "firstborn." Interestingly, this is a very common occurrence within the Biblical text such as we see with Jacob and Ephraim.

461. בְּכִי / 𐤁𐤊𐤉 / b-khi **Translation:** Weeping **Definition:** The act of expressing sorrow by shedding tears. **AHLB:** 1034-A (f) **Strong's:** 1065

462. בִּלְתִּי / 𐤁𐤋𐤕𐤉 / bil-ti **Translation:** Except **Definition:** With the exclusion of from the whole. The whole with the exception of one or more. **AHLB:** 2021 (ef) **Strong's:** 1115

463. בָּמָה / 𐤁𐤌𐤄 / ba-mah **Translation:** Platform **Definition:** A place higher than the surrounding area. **AHLB:** 1036-H (N) **Strong's:** 1116

464. בֵּן / 𐤁𐤍 / beyn **Translation:** Son **Definition:** A male offspring. This can be the son of the father or a later male descendant. One who continues the family line. **AHLB:** 1037-A (N) **Strong's:** 1121

More about the word בֵּן

In the original pictographic script, the first letter a picture of a tent or house. The second letter is the picture of a seed. The seed is a new generation of life that will grow and produce a new generation therefore, this letter can mean "to continue." When combined these two letters form the word meaning "to continue the house" and is the Hebrew word for a "son."

465. בַּעַל / / ba-al **Translation:** Master **Definition:** Having chief authority; a workman qualified to teach apprentices. **AHLB:** 2027 (N) **Strong's:** 1167

466. בָּקָר / / ba-qar **Translation:** Cattle **Definition:** Domesticated bovine animals. Strong beasts used to break the soil with plows. **AHLB:** 2035 (N) **Strong's:** 1241

467. בֹּקֶר / / bo-qer **Translation:** Morning **Definition:** The time from sunrise to noon. Breaking of daylight. **AHLB:** 2035 (g) **Strong's:** 1242

468. בָּרָד / / ba-rad **Translation:** Hailstones **Definition:** A precipitation in the form of irregular pellets or balls of ice. **AHLB:** 2037 (N) **Strong's:** 1259

469. בַּרְזֶל / / bar-zel **Translation:** Iron **Definition:** A heavy element frequently used in the making of weapons and tools. The most used of metals. **AHLB:** 3005 **Strong's:** 1270

470. בְּרִיחַ / / b-ri-ahh **Translation:** Wood bar **Definition:** Round wooden dowels. **AHLB:** 2038 (b) **Strong's:** 1280

471. בְּרִית / / b-rit **Translation:** Covenant **Definition:** A solemn and binding agreement between two or more parties especially for the performance of some action. Often instituted through a sacrifice. **AHLB:** 1043-H (N4) **Strong's:** 1285

More about the word בְּרִית

While the Hebrew word beriyt means "covenant" the cultural background of the word is helpful in understanding its full meaning. Beriyt comes from the parent root word bar meaning grain. Grains were fed to livestock to fatten them up to prepare them for the slaughter. Two other Hebrew words related to beriyt and also derived from the parent root bar can help understand the meaning of beriyt. The word beriy means fat and barut means meat. Notice the common theme with bar, beriy and barut, they all have to do with the slaughtering of livestock. The word beriyt is literally the animal that is slaughtered for the covenant ceremony. The phrase "make a covenant" is found thirteen times in the Hebrew Bible. In the Hebrew text this phrase is "karat beriyt". The word karat literally means "to cut". When a covenant is made a fattened animal is cut into pieces and laid out on the ground. Each party of the covenant then passes through the pieces signifying that if one of the parties fails to meet the agreement then the other has the right to do to the other what they did to the animal (see Genesis 15:10 and Jeremiah 34:18-20).

472. בֶּרֶךְ / [ancient Hebrew script] / b-rek **Translation:** Knee **Definition:** The joint between the femur and tibia of the leg. **AHLB:** 2039 (N) **Strong's:** 1290

473. בְּרָכָה / [illegible] / b-ra-khah **Translation:** Present **Definition:** A gift given to another in respect as if on bended knee. Also, a pool of water as a place where one kneels down to drink from. **AHLB:** 2039 (N1) **Strong's:** 1293

474. בֹּשֶׂם / [illegible] / bo-sem **Translation:** Sweet spice **Definition:** An aromatic spice that is pleasing to the nose. **AHLB:** 2024 (g) **Strong's:** 1314

475. בָּשָׂר / [illegible] / ba-sar **Translation:** Flesh **Definition:** The soft parts of a human or animal, composed primarily of skeletal muscle. Skin and muscle or the whole of the person. Meat as food. **AHLB:** 2025 (N) **Strong's:** 1320

More about the word בָּשָׂר

The verbal root of this word means "to bring good news." What does good news and flesh have in common? Flesh, or meat, was normally only eaten on very special occasions, a feast, the arrival of guests or whenever an event occurs that requires a celebration.

476. בֹּשֶׁת / [illegible] / bo-shet **Translation:** Shame **Definition:** A state of confusion in the sense of being dried up. **AHLB:** 1044-J (N2) **Strong's:** 1322

477. בַּת / [illegible] / bat **Translation:** Daughter **Definition:** A female having the relation of a child to parent. A village that resides outside of the city walls; as "the daughter of the city.". **AHLB:** 1037-A (N2) **Strong's:** 1323

478. בְּתוּלָה / b-tu-lah **Translation:** Virgin **Definition:** An unmarried young woman who is absolutely chaste. **AHLB:** 2045 (d1) **Strong's:** 1330

Gimel

479. גָּאוֹן / ga-on **Translation:** Majesty **Definition:** Elevated to a higher position. Supreme greatness or authority. **AHLB:** 1047-A (j) **Strong's:** 1347

480. גָּבוֹהַ / ga-vo-ah **Translation:** High **Definition:** Advanced in height such as a wall or hill. **AHLB:** 1048-H (c) **Strong's:** 1364

481. גְּבוּל / g-vul **Translation:** Border **Definition:** The outer edge of a region. Also the area within the borders. **AHLB:** 2049 (d) **Strong's:** 1366

482. גִּבּוֹר / gi-bor **Translation:** Courageous **Definition:** Having or characterized by mental or moral strength to venture, persevere, and withstand danger, fear or difficulty. **AHLB:** 2052 (ec) **Strong's:** 1368

483. גְּבוּרָה / g-vo-rah **Translation:** Bravery **Definition:** An act of defending one's property, convictions or beliefs. Control through physical strength. **AHLB:** 2052 (d1) **Strong's:** 1369

484. גִּבְעָה / giv-ah **Translation:** Knoll **Definition:** A small round hill. **AHLB:** 2051 (N1) **Strong's:** 1389

485. גֶּבֶר / / ge-ver **Translation:** Warrior **Definition:** One of great strength in battle, such as a warrior. One who is strong in authority, such as a master. **AHLB:** 2052 (N) **Strong's:** 1397

486. גָּג / / gag **Translation:** Roof **Definition:** The covering of a dwelling place. **AHLB:** 1049-A (N) **Strong's:** 1406

487. גְּדוּד / / g-dud **Translation:** Band **Definition:** A gathering of men for attacking or raiding. **AHLB:** 1050-B (d) **Strong's:** 1416

488. גָּדוֹל / / ga-dol **Translation:** Great **Definition:** Something with increased size, power or authority. **AHLB:** 2054 (c) **Strong's:** 1419

489. גּוֹי / / goy **Translation:** Nation **Definition:** A community of people of one or more nationalities and having a more or less defined territory and government. The people as the back, or body of the nation. **AHLB:** 1052-A (f) **Strong's:** 1471

490. גּוֹלָה / / go-lah **Translation:** Rising **Definition:** A rising of smoke from a burnt offering. Captivity in the sense of placing a yoke on the captives. **AHLB:** 1357-J (N1) **Strong's:** 1473

491. גּוֹרָל / / go-ral **Translation:** Lot **Definition:** Colored stones that are thrown and read to determine a course of action or to make a decision. **AHLB:** 2083 (g) **Strong's:** 1486

492. גַּיְא / / gai **Translation:** Valley **Definition:** An elongated depression between uplands, hills, or mountains. **AHLB:** 1047-M (N) **Strong's:** 1516

493. גַּל / / gal **Translation:** Mound **Definition:** An artificial hill or bank of earth or stones. A pile of rocks or soil. A spring gushing out of the ground. **AHLB:** 1058-A (N) **Strong's:** 1530

494. גִּלּוּל / / gi-lul **Translation:** Idol **Definition:** The image of a god made from wood or stone that is revered. **AHLB:** 1058-B (d) **Strong's:** 1544

495. גָּמָל / / ga-mal **Translation:** Camel **Definition:** Either of two ruminant mammals used as draft animals in the desert. The produce of the fields were tied in large bundles and transported on camels. **AHLB:** 2070 (N) **Strong's:** 1581

496. גַּן / / gan **Translation:** Garden **Definition:** A plot of ground where crops are grown. A place for growing crops, and often surrounded by a rock wall or hedge to protect it from grazing animals. **AHLB:** 1060-A (N) **Strong's:** 1588

497. גֶּפֶן / / ge-phen **Translation:** Grapevine **Definition:** A woody vine that usually climbs by tendrils and produces fruits that are grapes. **AHLB:** 2078 (N) **Strong's:** 1612

498. גֵּר / / ger **Translation:** Stranger **Definition:** A foreigner; a person or thing unknown or with whom one is unacquainted. **AHLB:** 1066-A (N) **Strong's:** 1616

499. גֹּרֶן / / go-ren **Translation:** Floor **Definition:** The level base of a room, barn or threshing floor. **AHLB:** 2085 (g) **Strong's:** 1637

500. גֶּשֶׁם / / ge-shem **Translation:** Rain shower **Definition:** The rain of the skies. **AHLB:** 2090 (N) **Strong's:** 1653

Dalet

501. דֶּבֶר / / de-ver **Translation:** Epidemic **Definition:** A wide spread disease effecting man or animal. A pestilence. **AHLB:** 2093 (N) **Strong's:** 1698

502. דָּבָר / / da-var **Translation:** Word **Definition:** An arrangement of words, ideas or concepts to form sentences. An action in the sense of acting out an arrangement. A plague as an act. **AHLB:** 2093 (N) **Strong's:** 1697

More about the word דָּבָר

The meaning of "words" are an ordered arrangement of words. Closely related to this word is the feminine word devorah, which is a bee. A bee hive is a colony of insects that live in a perfectly ordered society. Another closely related word is midbar, which is a wilderness. A wilderness is a place in perfect balance or order.

503. דְּבַשׁ / / d-vash **Translation:** Honey **Definition:** A sweet material elaborated out of the nectar of flowers in the honey sac of various bees. Also, dates as a thick, sticky and sweet food. **AHLB:** 2094 (N) **Strong's:** 1706

504. דָּגָן / 𐤃𐤂𐤍 / da-gan **Translation:** Cereal **Definition:** Relating to grain or plants that produce it. A plentiful crop. **AHLB:** 1072-A (m) **Strong's:** 1715

505. דּוֹד / 𐤃𐤅𐤃 / dod **Translation:** Beloved **Definition:** One who is cherished by another. **AHLB:** 1073-J (N) **Strong's:** 1730

506. דּוֹר / 𐤃𐤅𐤓 / dor **Translation:** Generation **Definition:** A body of living beings constituting a single step in the line of descent from an ancestor. **AHLB:** 1089-J (N) **Strong's:** 1755

507. דַּי / 𐤃𐤉 / dai **Translation:** Sufficient **Definition:** An amount that is not lacking. What is enough. **AHLB:** 1079-A (N) **Strong's:** 1767

508. דַּל / 𐤃𐤋 / dal **Translation:** Weak **Definition:** One who dangles the head in poverty or hunger. **AHLB:** 1081-A (N) **Strong's:** 1800

509. דֶּלֶת / 𐤃𐤋𐤕 / de-let **Translation:** Door **Definition:** A means of access; usually a swinging or sliding barrier by which an entry is closed and opened. **AHLB:** 1081-A (N2) **Strong's:** 1817

510. דָּם / 𐤃𐤌 / dam **Translation:** Blood **Definition:** The red fluid that circulates through body. **AHLB:** 1082-A (N) **Strong's:** 1818

511. דְּמוּת / 𐤃𐤌𐤅𐤕 / d-mut **Translation:** Likeness **Definition:** Copy; resemblance. The quality or state of being like something or someone else. **AHLB:** 1082-H (N^3) **Strong's:** 1823

512. דָּמַם / / da-mam **Translation:** Be silent **Definition:** To come to a standstill in speech or deed. To be quiet; refrain from speech or action. **AHLB:** 1082-B (N) **Strong's:** 1826

513. דַּעַת / / da-at **Translation:** Discernment **Definition:** The quality of being able to grasp and comprehend what is obscure. An intimacy with a person, idea or concept. **AHLB:** 1085-A (N2) **Strong's:** 1847

514. דֶּרֶךְ / / de-rek **Translation:** Road **Definition:** A route or path for traveled or walked. The path or manner of life. **AHLB:** 2112 (N) **Strong's:** 1870

Hey

515. הֶבֶל / / he-vel **Translation:** Vanity **Definition:** The state of being empty of contents or usefulness. **AHLB:** 1035-F (N) **Strong's:** 1892

516. הָדָר / / ha-dar **Translation:** Swell **Definition:** Someone or something that has been enlarged in size, pride or majesty. **AHLB:** 1089-F (N) **Strong's:** 1926

517. הוֹי / / hoi **Translation:** Ah **Definition:** An exclamation of surprise or pain. **AHLB:** 1102-J (N) **Strong's:** 1945

518. הוֹן / / hon **Translation:** Substance **Definition:** Foods or items of value. **AHLB:** 1106-J (N) **Strong's:** 1952

519. הֵיכָל / / hey-khal **Translation:** House **Definition:** The residence of a god (temple) or king (palace). **AHLB:** 1242-F (e) **Strong's:** 1964

520. הָמוֹן / / ha-mon **Translation:** Multitude **Definition:** A great number of people. A loud group. **AHLB:** 1105-A (j) **Strong's:** 1995

521. הַר / / har **Translation:** Hill **Definition:** A rounded natural elevation of land lower than a mountain. **AHLB:** 1112-A (N) **Strong's:** 2022

Zayin

522. זֶבַח / / z-vahh **Translation:** Sacrifice **Definition:** An animal killed for an offering. **AHLB:** 2117 (N) **Strong's:** 2077

523. זָהָב / / za-hav **Translation:** Gold **Definition:** A malleable yellow metallic element that is used especially in coins, jewelry, and dentures. A precious metal. **AHLB:** 1140-G (N) **Strong's:** 2091

524. זַיִת / / za-yit **Translation:** Olive **Definition:** The fruit or the tree. The fruit of the olive is used for food and as a source of oil. **AHLB:** 1160-M (N) **Strong's:** 2132

525. זָכָר / / za-khar **Translation:** Male **Definition:** Being the gender who begets offspring. One who acts and speaks for the family. **AHLB:** 2121 (N) **Strong's:** 2145

526. זִמָּה / zi-mah **Translation:** Mischief **Definition:** An annoying action resulting in grief, harm or evil. **AHLB:** 1151-A (N1) **Strong's:** 2154

527. זָקֵן / za-qeyn **Translation:** Beard **Definition:** The hair that grows on a man's face. A long beard as a sign of old age and wisdom. An elder as a bearded one. **AHLB:** 2132 (N) **Strong's:** 2205

528. זְרוֹעַ / z-ro-a **Translation:** Arm **Definition:** The human upper limb as representing power. **AHLB:** 2139 (c) **Strong's:** 2220

529. זֶרַע / ze-ra **Translation:** Seed **Definition:** The grains or ripened ovules of plants used for sowing. Scattered in the field to produce a crop. The singular word can be used for one or more. Also, the descendants of an individual, either male or female. **AHLB:** 2137 (N) **Strong's:** 2233

Hhet

530. חֶבֶל / hhe-vel **Translation:** Region **Definition:** An area surrounded by a specific border. **AHLB:** 2141 (N) **Strong's:** 2256

531. חָבַל / hha-val **Translation:** Take as a pledge **Definition:** To receive an object in exchange for a promise. **AHLB:** 2141 (V) **Strong's:** 2254

532. חַג / hhag **Translation:** Feast **Definition:** A commemoration of a special event with dancing, rejoicing, and sharing of food. A ceremony of joy and thanksgiving. A festival with a magnificent meal which is shared with a number of guests. **AHLB:** 1164-A (N) **Strong's:** 2282

533. חֶדֶר / / hhe-der **Translation:** Chamber **Definition:** A bedroom; a natural or artificial enclosed space or cavity. Place surrounded by walls. An inner place as hidden or secret. **AHLB:** 2150 (N) **Strong's:** 2315

534. חָדָשׁ / / hha-dash **Translation:** New **Definition:** Something that is new, renewed, restored or repaired. **AHLB:** 2151 (N) **Strong's:** 2319

535. חֹדֶשׁ / / hho-desh **Translation:** New moon **Definition:** The moon phase when the thin crescent first appears and is perceived as the renewal of the moon. The first day of the month. Also, a month as the interval between crescents. **AHLB:** 2151 (g) **Strong's:** 2320

536. חוֹמָה / / hho-mah **Translation:** Rampart **Definition:** A fortified enclosure. **AHLB:** 1174-J (N1) **Strong's:** 2346

537. חוּץ / / hhuts **Translation:** Outside **Definition:** A place or region beyond an enclosure or barrier. **AHLB:** 1179-J (N) **Strong's:** 2351

538. חָזוֹן / / hha-zon **Translation:** Vision **Definition:** To see or perceive what is normally not visible. **AHLB:** 1168-A (j) **Strong's:** 2377

539. חָזָק / / hha-zaq **Translation:** Forceful **Definition:** A strong grip on something to refrain or support. Driven with force. Acting with power. **AHLB:** 2152 (N) **Strong's:** 2389

540. חֵטְא / 𐤇𐤈𐤀 / hha-ta **Translation:** Fault **Definition:** A lack, weakness or failing; a mistake; the responsibility for wrongdoing. Missing of the target. A faulty one is one who has missed the target. **AHLB:** 1170-E (N) **Strong's:** 2399

541. חַטָּאָה / 𐤇𐤈𐤀𐤄 / hha-ta-a **Translation:** Error **Definition:** An act or condition of ignorant or imprudent deviation from a code of behavior. A missing of the target in the sense of making a mistake. The sacrifice, which by transference, becomes the sin. **AHLB:** 1170-E (N1) **Strong's:** 2403

542. חִטָּה / 𐤇𐤉𐤈𐤄 / hhi-tah **Translation:** Wheat **Definition:** A cereal grain that yields a fine white flour, the chief ingredient of bread. **AHLB:** 2177 (e1) **Strong's:** 2406

543. חַי / 𐤇𐤉 / hhai **Translation:** Life **Definition:** The quality that distinguishes a vital and functional being from a dead body. Literally the stomach. Also, used idiomatically of living creatures, especially in conjunction with land, ground or field. **AHLB:** 1171-A (N) **Strong's:** 2416

More about the word חַי

The Hebrew word hhai is usually translated as life. In the Hebrew language all words are related to something concrete or physical, something that can be observed by one of the five senses. Some examples of concrete words would be tree, water, hot, sweet or loud. The western Greek mind frequently uses abstracts or mental words to convey ideas. An abstract word is something that cannot be sensed by the five senses. Some examples would be bless, believe, and the word life. Whenever working with an abstract word in the Biblical text it will help to uncover the concrete background to the word for proper interpretation. How did the ancient Hebrew perceive "life?" A clue can be found in Job 38:39, "Will you hunt prey for the lion and will you fill the stomach of the young lion?" In this verse the word "stomach" is the Hebrew word hhai. What does the stomach have to do with life? In our culture it is very uncommon for anyone to experience true hunger but this was an all too often experience for the Ancient Hebrews. To the Ancient Hebrews life is seen as a full stomach while an empty stomach is seen as death.

544. חַיִל / [illegible] / hha-yil **Translation:** Force **Definition:** The pressure exerted to make a piercing. **AHLB:** 1173-M (N) **Strong's:** 2428

545. חִיצוֹן / [illegible] / hhi-tson **Translation:** Outside **Definition:** What is outward or external. Also the idea of secular as being outside. **AHLB:** 1179-M (j) **Strong's:** 2435

546. חֵיק / [illegible] / hheyq **Translation:** Bosom **Definition:** The human chest, especially the front side. **AHLB:** 1163-M (N) **Strong's:** 2436

547. חָכָם / [illegible] / hha-kham **Translation:** Skilled one **Definition:** A person characterized by a deep understanding of a craft. **AHLB:** 2159 (N) **Strong's:** 2450

548. חָכְמָה / / hhakh-mah **Translation:** Skill **Definition:** The ability to decide or discern between good and bad, right and wrong. **AHLB:** 2159 (N1) **Strong's:** 2451

549. חֵלֶב / / hhe-lev **Translation:** Fat **Definition:** Animal tissue consisting of cells distended with greasy or oily matter; adipose tissue. The fat of an animal as the choicest part. **AHLB:** 2160 (N) **Strong's:** 2459

550. חָלָב / / hha-lav **Translation:** Milk **Definition:** A white fatty liquid secreted by cows, sheep and goats, and used for food or as a source of butter, cheeses, yogurt, etc. **AHLB:** 2160 (N) **Strong's:** 2461

551. חֲלוֹם / / hha-lom **Translation:** Dream **Definition:** A series of thoughts, images or emotions occurring during sleep. **AHLB:** 2164 (c) **Strong's:** 2472

552. חַלּוֹן / / hha-lon **Translation:** Window **Definition:** A hole in the wall that admits light and a view of the other side. **AHLB:** 1173-A (j) **Strong's:** 2474

553. חָלָל / / hha-lal **Translation:** Pierced **Definition:** Having holes. **AHLB:** 1173-B (N) **Strong's:** 2491

554. חֵלֶק / / hhey-leq **Translation:** Portion **Definition:** An individual-s part or share of something. The portions dispersed out. **AHLB:** 2167 (N) **Strong's:** 2506

555. חֶלְקָה / / hhel-qah **Translation:** Smooth **Definition:** Having an even, continuous surface. This word can also mean "flattery" in the sense of being slippery. **AHLB:** 2167 (N1) **Strong's:** 2513

556. חֶמְדָּה / / hhem-dah **Translation:** Pleasant **Definition:** Having qualities that tend to give pleasure. An object of desire. **AHLB:** 2169 (N^1) **Strong's:** 2532

557. חֵמָה / / hhey-mah **Translation:** Fury **Definition:** Intense, disordered, and often destructive rage. An intense heat from anger. **AHLB:** 1174-A (N1) **Strong's:** 2534

558. חֲמוֹר / / hha-mor **Translation:** Donkey **Definition:** A male ass. **AHLB:** 2175 (c) **Strong's:** 2543

559. חָמָס / / hha-mas **Translation:** Violence **Definition:** Exertion of physical force so as to injure or abuse. A violent shaking. **AHLB:** 2172 (N) **Strong's:** 2555

560. חֹמֶר / / hha-mor **Translation:** Mortar **Definition:** A thick and slimy soil used to join bricks together or for making bricks. **AHLB:** 2175 (g) **Strong's:** 2563

561. חֵן / / hheyn **Translation:** Beauty **Definition:** The qualities in a person or thing that give pleasure to the senses. Someone or something that is desired, approved, favored or in agreement by another. **AHLB:** 1175-A (N) **Strong's:** 2580

562. חֲנִית / / hha-nit **Translation:** Spear **Definition:** A long shaft with a pointed tip and used as a weapon. A tent pole which may also be used as a spear. **AHLB:** 1175-A (N4) **Strong's:** 2595

563. חִנָּם / / hhi-nam **Translation:** Freely **Definition:** Having no restrictions. A work or action that is performed without wages or without cause. **AHLB:** 1175-A (p) **Strong's:** 2600

564. חֶסֶד / / hhe-sed **Translation:** Kindness **Definition:** Of a sympathetic nature; quality or state of being sympathetic. In the sense of bowing the neck to another as a sign of kindness. **AHLB:** 2181 (N) **Strong's:** 2617

565. חָסִיד / / hha-sid **Translation:** Kind one **Definition:** One who shows favor, mercy or compassion to another. **AHLB:** 2181 (b) **Strong's:** 2623

566. חֵפֶץ / / hhey-phets **Translation:** Delight **Definition:** An object or action that one desires. **AHLB:** 2191 (N) **Strong's:** 2656

567. חֵץ / / hheyts **Translation:** Arrow **Definition:** A missile weapon shot from a bow having a pointed head, slender shaft and feathers as a butt. **AHLB:** 1179-A (N) **Strong's:** 2671

568. חֲצוֹצְרָה / / hha-tsots-rah **Translation:** Trumpet **Definition:** A loud wind instrument. **AHLB:** 3018 **Strong's:** 2689

569. חֲצִי / / hha-tsi **Translation:** Half **Definition:** An equal part of something divided into two pieces. **AHLB:** 1179-A (f) **Strong's:** 2677

570. חָצֵר / / hha-tser **Translation:** Yard **Definition:** The grounds of a building or group of buildings. Villages outside of the larger cities, as "the yard of the city." A courtyard as outside the house. **AHLB:** 2197 (N) **Strong's:** 2691

571. חֹק / / hhuq **Translation:** Custom **Definition:** A usage or practice common to many or to a particular place or class or habitual with an individual. **AHLB:** 1180-J (N) **Strong's:** 2706

572. חֻקָּה / [pictograph] / hhuq-qah **Translation:** Ritual **Definition:** A repeating of the same actions. A custom. **AHLB:** 1180-J (N1) **Strong's:** 2708

573. חֶרֶב / [pictograph] / hhe-rev **Translation:** Sword **Definition:** A weapon with a long blade for cutting or thrusting. **AHLB:** 2199 (N) **Strong's:** 2719

574. חָרְבָּה / [pictograph] / hhar-bah **Translation:** Wasteland **Definition:** Barren or uncultivated land. Also a dry land. **AHLB:** 2199 (N1) **Strong's:** 2723

575. חָרוֹן / [pictograph] / hha-ron **Translation:** Burning wrath **Definition:** A fierce anger. **AHLB:** 1181-A (j) **Strong's:** 2740

576. חֵרֶם / [pictograph] / hhey-rem **Translation:** Net **Definition:** Something filled with holes or is perforated. Also something accursed in the sense of being filled with holes. **AHLB:** 2206 (N) **Strong's:** 2764

577. חרם / [pictograph] / hha-ram **Translation:** Perforate **Definition:** To be filled with holes. **AHLB:** 2206 (V) **Strong's:** 2763

578. חֶרְפָּה / [pictograph] / hher-pah **Translation:** Disgrace **Definition:** A scorn, taunting or reproach as a piercing. **AHLB:** 2208 (N1) **Strong's:** 2781

579. חָרָשׁ / [pictograph] / hha-rash **Translation:** Engraver **Definition:** A sculptor or carver who engraves wood, stone or metal. **AHLB:** 2211 (N) **Strong's:** 2796

580. חֹשֶׁךְ / hho-shekh **Translation:** Darkness **Definition:** The state of being dark. As the darkness of a moonless night. **AHLB:** 2215 (g) **Strong's:** 2822

581. חֹשֶׁן / hho-shen **Translation:** Breastplate **Definition:** An ornamental plate worn by the High Priest that held stones representing the twelve tribes of Israel and the Urim and Thummim. **AHLB:** 1182-J (m) **Strong's:** 2833

Tet

582. טַבָּח / ta-bahh **Translation:** Slaughtering **Definition:** The act of slaughtering, the meat of the slaughter or one who slaughters. Also an executioner as one who slaughters. **AHLB:** 2227 (N) **Strong's:** 2876

583. טַבַּעַת / ta-ba-at **Translation:** Ring **Definition:** A circular band of metal or other durable material. Also the signet ring containing the mark of the owner that is sunk into a lump of clay as a seal. **AHLB:** 2229 (N2) **Strong's:** 2885

584. טָהוֹר / ta-hor **Translation:** Pure **Definition:** Unmixed with any other matter. A man, animal or object that is free of impurities or is not mixed. **AHLB:** 1204-G (c) **Strong's:** 2889

585. טוֹב / tov **Translation:** Functional **Definition:** Fulfilling the action for which a person or thing is specially fitted or used, or for which a thing exists. Something that functions within its intended purpose. **AHLB:** 1186-J (N) **Strong's:** 2896

More about the word טוב

The first use of this word is in Genesis chapter one where Elohiym calls his handiwork "good" (as it is usually translated). It should always be remembered that the Hebrews often relate descriptions to functionality. When Elohiym looked at his handiwork, he did not see that it was "good," he saw that it was functional-"like a well oiled and tuned machine."

586. טוּב / ⌂Y⊗ / tuv **Translation:** Goods **Definition:** Items, produce or other essentials needed for survival. **AHLB:** 1186-J (N) **Strong's:** 2898

587. טַל / J⊗ / tal **Translation:** Dew **Definition:** Moisture condensed on the surfaces of cool bodies or objects, especially at night. **AHLB:** 1196-A (N) **Strong's:** 2919

588. טָמֵא / ᗢ~~⊗ / ta-mey **Translation:** Unclean **Definition:** What is morally or physically impure; dirty, filthy. **AHLB:** 1197-E (N) **Strong's:** 2931

589. טֻמְאָה / ᛉᗢ~~Y⊗ / tum-ah **Translation:** Unclean **Definition:** What is morally or physically impure; dirty, filthy. **AHLB:** 1197-E (o1) **Strong's:** 2932

590. טַף / / taph **Translation:** Children **Definition:** The offspring of the parent or descendents of a patron. More than one child. **AHLB:** 1201-A (N) **Strong's:** 2945

Yud

591. יְאוֹר / / y-or **Translation:** Stream **Definition:** A body of running water; any body of flowing water. **AHLB:** 1227-D (N) **Strong's:** 2975

592. יָד / / yad **Translation:** Hand **Definition:** The terminal, functional part of the forelimb. Hand with the ability to work, throw and give thanks. **AHLB:** 1211-A (N) **Strong's:** 3027

593. יוֹבֵל / / yo-veyl **Translation:** Trumpet **Definition:** An instrument of flowing air to make a sound. Also, the horn of a ram as used as a trumpet. **AHLB:** 1035-L (g) **Strong's:** 3104

594. יוֹם / / yom **Translation:** Day **Definition:** The time of light between one night and the next one. Usually in the context of daylight hours but may also refer to the entire day or even a season. **AHLB:** 1220-J (N) **Strong's:** 3117

595. יוֹמָם / / yo-mam **Translation:** Daytime **Definition:** The time of the day when the sun is shining. **AHLB:** 1220-J (p) **Strong's:** 3119

596. יוֹנָה / / yo-nah **Translation:** Dove **Definition:** Any of numerous species of birds, especially a small wild one. **AHLB:** 1221-J (N1) **Strong's:** 3123

597. יַחַד / / ya-hhad **Translation:** Together **Definition:** In or into one place, mass, collection, or group. **AHLB:** 1165-L (N) **Strong's:** 3162

598. יַיִן / / ya-yin **Translation:** Wine **Definition:** Fermented juice of fresh grapes. From the mire in the wine. **AHLB:** 1221-M (N) **Strong's:** 3196

599. יֶלֶד / / ye-led **Translation:** Boy **Definition:** A male child from birth to puberty. **AHLB:** 1257-L (N) **Strong's:** 3206

600. יָם / / yam **Translation:** Sea **Definition:** A large body of water. Also, the direction of the great sea (the Mediterranean), the west. **AHLB:** 1220-A (N) **Strong's:** 3220

601. יָמִין / / ya-min **Translation:** Right hand **Definition:** The hand on the right side of a person. Also, a direction as in to the right. **AHLB:** 1290-L (b) **Strong's:** 3225

602. יְמָנִי / / y-ma-ni **Translation:** Right **Definition:** A direction as in to the right. **AHLB:** 1290-L (f) **Strong's:** 3233

603. יעץ / / ya-ats **Translation:** Give advice **Definition:** To assist another by providing wise counsel. **AHLB:** 1363-L (V) **Strong's:** 3289

604. יַעַר / / ya-ar **Translation:** Forest **Definition:** A dark place dense with trees. **AHLB:** 1526-L (N) **Strong's:** 3293

605. יָפֶה / / ya-pheh **Translation:** Beautiful **Definition:** Generally pleasing. Possessing the qualities of loveliness or functionality. **AHLB:** 1224-H (N) **Strong's:** 3303

606. יָקָר / / ya-qar **Translation:** Valuable **Definition:** Having qualities worthy of respect, admiration, or esteem **AHLB:** 1434-L (N) **Strong's:** 3368

607. יָרֵא / / ya-rey **Translation:** Fearful **Definition:** Full of fear or dread. **AHLB:** 1227-E (N) **Strong's:** 3373

608. יִרְאָה / / yir-ah **Translation:** Fearfulness **Definition:** Inclined to be afraid. **AHLB:** 1227-E (N1) **Strong's:** 3374

609. יָרֵחַ / / ya-rey-ahh **Translation:** Moon **Definition:** The second brightest object in the sky which reflects the sun's light. Also, a month by counting its cycles. **AHLB:** 1445-L (N) **Strong's:** 3394

610. יְרִיעָה / / y-ri-ah **Translation:** Tent wall **Definition:** The goat hair curtain that forms the walls of the tent. **AHLB:** 1440-L (N) **Strong's:** 3407

611. יָרֵךְ / / ya-rey-akh **Translation:** Midsection **Definition:** The lower abdomen and back. **AHLB:** 1448-L (N) **Strong's:** 3409

612. יַרְכָה / / yar-khah **Translation:** Flank **Definition:** The hollow of the loins between the legs. **AHLB:** 1448-L (N1) **Strong's:** 3411

613. יֵשׁ / / yeysh **Translation:** There is **Definition:** Something that exists. **AHLB:** 1228-A (N) **Strong's:** 3426

614. יְשׁוּעָה / / y-shu-ah **Translation:** Relief **Definition:** A deliverance or freedom from a trouble, burden or danger. **AHLB:** 1476-L (d1) **Strong's:** 3444

615. יֶשַׁע / / ye-sha **Translation:** Rescue **Definition:** A deliverance or freedom from a burden, enemy or trouble. **AHLB:** 1476-L (N) **Strong's:** 3468

616. יָשָׁר / / ya-shar **Translation:** Straight **Definition:** Without a bend, angle, or curve. A straight line, path or thought. The cord of the bow as stretched taught. **AHLB:** 1480-L (N) **Strong's:** 3477

617. יָתוֹם / / ya-tom **Translation:** Orphan **Definition:** Having no mother or father. **AHLB:** 1496-L (c) **Strong's:** 3490

618. יֶתֶר / / ye-ter **Translation:** Remainder **Definition:** A remaining group, part or trace. **AHLB:** 1480-L (N) **Strong's:** 3499

Kaph

619. כָּבֵד / / ka-veyd **Translation:** Heavy **Definition:** Having great weight. Something that is weighty. May also be grief or sadness in the sense of heaviness. Also, the liver as the heaviest of the organs. **AHLB:** 2246 (N) **Strong's:** 3515

620. כָּבוֹד / / ka-vod **Translation:** Armament **Definition:** The arms and equipment of a soldier or military unit. **AHLB:** 2246 (c) **Strong's:** 3519

More about the word כָּבוֹד

In Exodus 16:7 we read "and in the morning you shall see the glory of the LORD" (RSV). What is the "glory" of YHWH? First we must recognize that the "glory" is something that will be seen. Secondly, the word "glory" is an abstract word. If we look at how this word is paralleled with other words in poetical passages of the Bible, we can discover the original concrete meaning of this word. In Psalm 3:3 the kavod of Elohiym is paralleled with his shield and in Job 29:20, Job's kavod is paralleled with his bow. In Psalm 24:8 we read "who is this king of the kavod, YHWH is strong and mighty, YHWH is mighty in battle." The original concrete meaning of kavod is battle armaments. This meaning of "armament" fits with the literal meaning of the root of kavod, which is "heavy," as armaments are the heavy weapons and defenses of battle. In the Exodus 16:7, Israel will "see" the "armament" of YHWH, the one who has done battle for them with the Egyptians.

621. כֶּבֶשׂ / כבש / ke-ves **Translation:** Sheep **Definition:** A mammal related to the goat domesticated for its flesh and wool. **AHLB:** 2273 (N) **Strong's:** 3532

622. כֹּהֵן / כהן / ko-heyn **Translation:** Administrator **Definition:** One who manages the affairs and activities of an organization. The administrators (often translated as "priest") of Israel are Levites who manage the Tent of Meeting, and later the Temple, as well as teach the people the teachings and directions of YHWH, and perform other duties, such as the inspection of people and structures for disease. **AHLB:** 1244-G (g) **Strong's:** 3548

More about the word כֹּהֵן

While the priests of Israel were the religious leaders of the community this is not the meaning of the word kohen. The Hebrew word for the priests of other nations is komer from a root meaning burn and may be in reference to the priests who burn children in the fires of Molech (2 Kings 23:10). The word kohen comes from a root meaning a base such as the base of a column. The koheniym (plural of kohen) are the structural support of the community. It is their responsibility to keep the community standing tall and straight, a sign of righteousness.

623. כּוֹכָב / ⵎШYШ / ko-khav **Translation:** Star **Definition:** A natural luminous body visible in the night sky. **AHLB:** 1232-B (g) **Strong's:** 3556

624. כּוֹל / ᒍYШ / kol **Translation:** All **Definition:** The whole of a group. **AHLB:** 1242-J (N) **Strong's:** 3605

625. כּוֹס / ≢YШ / kos **Translation:** Cup **Definition:** A vessel for holding liquids, usually for drinking. **AHLB:** 1245-J (N) **Strong's:** 3563

626. כָּזָב / כזב / ka-zav **Translation:** Lie **Definition:** A false or vain report. **AHLB:** 2253 (N) **Strong's:** 3577

627. כֹּחַ / כח / ko-ahh **Translation:** Strength **Definition:** The quality or state of being strong. **AHLB:** 1238-J (N) **Strong's:** 3581

628. כִּי / כי / ki **Translation:** Given that **Definition:** Prone or disposed to according to what preceded. A reference to the previous or following context. **AHLB:** 1240-A (N) **Strong's:** 3588

629. כִּיכָּר / כיכר / ki-kar **Translation:** Roundness **Definition:** Cylindrical; something as a circle, globe or ring that is round. A round thing or place. A coin as a round piece of gold or silver. A round loaf of bread. The plain, as a round piece of land. **AHLB:** 2258 (e) **Strong's:** 3603

630. כֶּלֶב / כלב / ke-lev **Translation:** Dog **Definition:** An unclean four-footed animal. Also meaning contempt or reproach. **AHLB:** 2259 (N) **Strong's:** 3611

631. כַּלָּה / כלה / ka-lah **Translation:** Daughter-in-law **Definition:** The wife of one's son. Bride of the son, as brought into the camp, in the sense of making the man complete. **AHLB:** 1242-B (N1) **Strong's:** 3618

632. כְּלִי / כלי / k-li **Translation:** Item **Definition:** A utensil or implement usually for carrying or storing various materials. **AHLB:** 1242-A (f) **Strong's:** 3627

633. כִּלְיָה / כליה / kil-yah **Translation:** Kidney **Definition:** An organ of the body. The seat of emotion in Hebraic thought. **AHLB:** 1242-A (f1) **Strong's:** 3629

634. כְּלִמָּה / / k-li-mah **Translation:** Shame **Definition:** The painful feeling of something dishonorable, improper, ridiculous, done by oneself or another. **AHLB:** 2261 (b1) **Strong's:** 3639

635. כִּנּוֹר / / ki-nor **Translation:** Harp **Definition:** A plucked stringed musical instrument; **AHLB:** 2270 (ec) **Strong's:** 3658

636. כָּנָף / / ka-naph **Translation:** Wing **Definition:** An appendage that allows an animal, bird or insect to fly. Also, the wings of a garment. **AHLB:** 2269 (N) **Strong's:** 3671

637. כִּסֵּא / / ki-sey **Translation:** Seat **Definition:** A special chair of one in eminence. Usually a throne or seat of authority. **AHLB:** 1245-E (e) **Strong's:** 3678

638. כְּסִיל / / k-sil **Translation:** Fool **Definition:** One who has confidence in something vain or empty. **AHLB:** 2275 (b) **Strong's:** 3684

639. כֶּסֶף / / ke-seph **Translation:** Silver **Definition:** A soft metal capable of a high degree of polish used for coinage, implements and ornaments. A desired and precious metal. **AHLB:** 2277 (N) **Strong's:** 3701

640. כַּף / / kaph **Translation:** Palm **Definition:** A tropical tree with fan-shaped leaves. Part of the hand or foot between the base of the digits and the wrist or ankle. A palm-shaped object. **AHLB:** 1247-A (N) **Strong's:** 3709

641. כְּפִיר / / k-phir **Translation:** Cub **Definition:** A young lion. Also, a "village". **AHLB:** 2283 (b) **Strong's:** 3715

642. כַּפֹּרֶת / 𐤊𐤐𐤅𐤓𐤕 / ka-po-ret **Translation:** Lid **Definition:** The cover of a box or other container. **AHLB:** 2283 (c2) **Strong's:** 3727

643. כְּרוּב / 𐤊𐤓𐤅𐤁 / k-ruv **Translation:** Keruv **Definition:** A supernatural creature, identified in other Semitic cultures as a winged lion, a Griffin. **AHLB:** n/a **Strong's:** 3742

644. כֶּרֶם / 𐤊𐤓𐤌 / k-rem **Translation:** Vineyard **Definition:** A planting of grapevines. **AHLB:** 2288 (N) **Strong's:** 3754

645. כְּתֹנֶת / 𐤊𐤕𐤅𐤍𐤕 / k-to-net **Translation:** Tunic **Definition:** A simple slip-on garment with or without sleeves. **AHLB:** 2298 (c2) **Strong's:** 3801

646. כָּתֵף / 𐤊𐤕𐤐 / ka-teyph **Translation:** Shoulder piece **Definition:** The part of an object that acts like a shoulder. **AHLB:** 2299 (N) **Strong's:** 3802

Lamed

647. לְאוֹם / 𐤋𐤀𐤅𐤌 / l-om **Translation:** Community **Definition:** A unified body of individuals; a group of people bound together. **AHLB:** 1266-D (c) **Strong's:** 3816

648. לֵב / 𐤋𐤁 / leyv **Translation:** Heart **Definition:** Literally, the vital organ which pumps blood, but, also seen as the seat of thought; the mind. **AHLB:** 1255-A (N) **Strong's:** 3820

More about the word לֵב

To the ancient Hebrews the heart was the mind, the thoughts. When we are told to love Elohiym with all our heart (Deut 6:5) it is not speaking of an emotional love, but to keep our minds and our thoughts working for him. The first picture in this Hebrew word is a shepherd staff and represents authority, as the shepherd has authority over his flock. The second letter is the picture of the floor plan of the nomadic tent and represents the idea of being inside, as the family resides within the tent. When combined they mean "the authority within".

649. לֵבָב / 𐤋𐤁𐤁 / ley-vav **Translation:** Heart **Definition:** Literally, the vital organ which pumps blood, but, also seen as the seat of thought; the mind. **AHLB:** 1255-B (N) **Strong's:** 3824

650. לְבוּשׁ / 𐤋𐤁𐤅𐤔 / l-vush **Translation:** Clothing **Definition:** Garments in general. **AHLB:** 2304 (d) **Strong's:** 3830

651. לָבָן / 𐤋𐤁𐤍 / la-van **Translation:** White **Definition:** Free from color. **AHLB:** 2303 (N) **Strong's:** 3836

652. לוּחַ / 𐤋𐤅𐤇 / lu-ahh **Translation:** Slab **Definition:** A wood or stone tablet or plank. Often used for writing. **AHLB:** 1261-J (N) **Strong's:** 3871

653. לֶחֶם / / le-hhem **Translation:** Bread **Definition:** Baked and leavened food primarily made of flour or meal. **AHLB:** 2305 (N) **Strong's:** 3899

654. לַיִל / / la-yil **Translation:** Night **Definition:** The time from dusk to dawn. The hours associated with darkness and sleep. **AHLB:** 1265-M (N) **Strong's:** 3915

655. לְעֻמַּת / / l-u-mat **Translation:** Alongside **Definition:** To stand with, or next to, someone or something. **AHLB:** 1358-J (N2) **Strong's:** 5980

656. לָשׁוֹן / / la-shon **Translation:** Tongue **Definition:** A fleshy moveable process on the floor of the mouth used in speaking and eating. Also, language as a tongue. **AHLB:** 2325 (c) **Strong's:** 3956

657. לִשְׁכָּה / / lish-kah **Translation:** Chamber **Definition:** A room or open area within a structure. **AHLB:** 2323 (e1) **Strong's:** 3957

Mem

658. מְאֹד / / m-od **Translation:** Many **Definition:** A large but indefinite number. An abundance of things (many, much, great), actions (complete, wholly, strong, quick) or character (very). **AHLB:** 1004-J (k) **Strong's:** 3966

659. מְאוּמָה / / m-u-mah **Translation:** Anything **Definition:** An indeterminate amount or thing. **AHLB:** 1289-D (d1) **Strong's:** 3972

660. מַאֲכָל / / ma-a-kal **Translation:** Nourishment **Definition:** Food; nutriment. For giving sustenance and making one whole. **AHLB:** 1242-C (a) **Strong's:** 3978

661. מִבְצָר / / miv-tsar **Translation:** Fence **Definition:** A walled place of protection and confinement. **AHLB:** 2033 (h) **Strong's:** 4013

662. מִגְדָּל / / mig-dal **Translation:** Tower **Definition:** A structure higher than its diameter and high relative to its surroundings. Place of great size. **AHLB:** 2054 (h) **Strong's:** 4026

663. מָגֵן / / ma-geyn **Translation:** Shield **Definition:** A broad piece of defensive armor carried on the arm. A protective structure. Wall of protection. **AHLB:** 1060-A (a) **Strong's:** 4043

664. מַגֵּפָה / / ma-gey-phah **Translation:** Pestilence **Definition:** A plague or other disaster that smites people or beasts. **AHLB:** 2377 (k^1) **Strong's:** 4046

665. מִגְרָשׁ / / mig-rash **Translation:** Pasture **Definition:** A place for grazing livestock, usually on the outskirts of a village or city. **AHLB:** 2089 (h1) **Strong's:** 4054

666. מִדְבָּר / / mid-bar **Translation:** Wilderness **Definition:** A tract or region uncultivated and uninhabited by human beings. Place of order, a sanctuary. **AHLB:** 2093 (h) **Strong's:** 4057

More about the word מִדְבָּר

For forty years Elohiym had Israel wander in the "wilderness." Insights into why Elohiym had chosen the wilderness for their wanderings can be found in the roots of this word. The root word is "davar" and is most frequently translated as "speak," but more literally means to "order" or "arrange" words. The word "midbar" is a place existing in a perfectly arranged order, an ecosystem in harmony and balance. By placing Israel in this environment he is teaching them balance, order and harmony.

667. מִדָּה / 𐤌𐤃𐤄 / mi-dah **Translation:** Measurement **Definition:** A size or distance that is determined by comparing to a standard of measure. **AHLB:** 1280-A (N1) **Strong's:** 4060

668. מְדִינָה / 𐤌𐤃𐤉𐤍𐤄 / m-di-nah **Translation:** Province **Definition:** The jurisdiction of responsibility of a judge or lord. **AHLB:** 1083-M (k1) **Strong's:** 4082

669. מוּל / 𐤌𐤅𐤋 / mul **Translation:** Forefront **Definition:** In front of or at the head of, in space or time. **AHLB:** 1288-J (N) **Strong's:** 4136

670. מוּסָר / 𐤌𐤅𐤎𐤓 / mu-sar **Translation:** Instruction **Definition:** Knowledge, information or example imparted to provide guidance, correction and discipline. **AHLB:** 1342-L (a) **Strong's:** 4148

671. מוֹעֵד / 𐤌𐤅𐤏𐤃 / mo-eyd **Translation:** Appointed **Definition:** Persons, places or things that are fixed or officially set. **AHLB:** 1349-L (a) **Strong's:** 4150

672. מוֹפֵת / / mo-phet **Translation:** Wonder **Definition:** An amazing sight or event that causes one to be dismayed. Something out of the ordinary. **AHLB:** 1390-L (a) **Strong's:** 4159

673. מוֹצָא / / mo-tsa **Translation:** Going out **Definition:** Coming or issuing out, such as a spring or words from the mouth. **AHLB:** 1392-L (a) **Strong's:** 4161

674. מוֹקֵשׁ / / mo-qeysh **Translation:** Snare **Definition:** A trap laid with bait to capture an animal or person. An entrapment. **AHLB:** 2132 (V) **Strong's:** 4170

675. מוֹשָׁב / / mo-shav **Translation:** Settling **Definition:** The place of sitting, resting or dwelling, usually temporarily. **AHLB:** 1462-L (a) **Strong's:** 4186

676. מָוֶת / / ma-wet **Translation:** Death **Definition:** A permanent cessation of all vital functions; the end of life. **AHLB:** 1298-J (N) **Strong's:** 4194

677. מִזְבֵּחַ / / miz-bey-ahh **Translation:** Altar **Definition:** The place of sacrifice. **AHLB:** 2117 (h) **Strong's:** 4196

678. מִזְמוֹר / / miz-mor **Translation:** Melody **Definition:** A musical composition plucked on a musical instrument. A song set to music. **AHLB:** 2124 (hc) **Strong's:** 4210

679. מִזְרָח / / miz-rah **Translation:** Sunrise **Definition:** When the first light of the sun comes over the horizon. An eastward direction as the place of the rising sun. **AHLB:** 2135 (h) **Strong's:** 4217

680. מִזְרָק / 𐤌𐤆𐤓𐤒 / miz-raq **Translation:** Sprinkling basin **Definition:** A container of liquid that is used to drip the liquid. **AHLB:** 2138 (h) **Strong's:** 4219

681. מַחֲלְקָה / 𐤌𐤇𐤋𐤒𐤄 / ma-hhal-qah **Translation:** Portion **Definition:** The part received from what was divided. **AHLB:** 2167 (a2) **Strong's:** 4256

682. מַחֲנֶה / 𐤌𐤇𐤍𐤄 / ma-hha-neh **Translation:** Campsite **Definition:** A place suitable for or used as the location of a camp. The inhabitants of a camp. **AHLB:** 1175-H (a) **Strong's:** 4264

683. מָחָר / 𐤌𐤀𐤇𐤓 / ma-hhar **Translation:** Tomorrow **Definition:** The next day. At a time following. **AHLB:** 1181-A (a) **Strong's:** 4279

684. מָחֳרָת / 𐤌𐤀𐤇𐤓𐤕 / ma-hha-rat **Translation:** Morrow **Definition:** The next day. At a time following. **AHLB:** 1181-A (a2) **Strong's:** 4283

685. מַחֲשָׁבָה / 𐤌𐤇𐤔𐤁𐤄 / ma-hha-sha-vah **Translation:** Invention **Definition:** A product of the imagination. Designing or planning of inventions or plans. **AHLB:** 2213 (a1) **Strong's:** 4284

686. מִטָּה / 𐤌𐤍𐤈𐤄 / mi-tah **Translation:** Bed **Definition:** A place for sleeping. Spread out sheet for sleeping. **AHLB:** 1308-A (h1) **Strong's:** 4296

687. מַטֶּה / 𐤌𐤈𐤄 / mat-teh **Translation:** Branch **Definition:** A branch used as a staff. Also, a tribe as a branch of the family. **AHLB:** 1285-H (N) **Strong's:** 4294

688. מָטָר / / ma-tar **Translation:** Precipitation **Definition:** A rain, snow or exceptionally heavy dew. **AHLB:** 2336 (N) **Strong's:** 4306

689. מַיִם / / ma-yim **Translation:** Water **Definition:** The Liquid of streams, ponds and seas or stored in cisterns or jars. The necessary liquid that is drank. **AHLB:** 1281-A (N) **Strong's:** 4325

690. מִין / / min **Translation:** Kind **Definition:** A category of creature that comes from its own kind as a firm rule. **AHLB:** 1290-M (N) **Strong's:** 4327

691. מַכָּה / / ma-kah **Translation:** Crushed **Definition:** Pressed or squeezed with a force that destroys or deforms. Also a plague. **AHLB:** 1310-A (a1) **Strong's:** 4347

692. מְלֹא / / m-lo **Translation:** Filling **Definition:** An act or instance of filling; something used to fill a cavity, container, or depression. **AHLB:** 1288-E (c) **Strong's:** 4393

693. מָלֵא / / ma-ley **Translation:** Full **Definition:** Containing as much or as many as is possible or normal. **AHLB:** 1288-E (N) **Strong's:** 4392

694. מַלְאָךְ / / mal-akh **Translation:** Messenger **Definition:** One who bears a message or runs an errand. Walks for another. **AHLB:** 1264-D (a) **Strong's:** 4397

695. מְלָאכָה / / m-la-khah **Translation:** Business **Definition:** The principal occupation of one's life. A service. **AHLB:** 1264-D (k1) **Strong's:** 4399

696. מִלָּה / מלה / mi-lah **Translation:** Comment **Definition:** A word or speech as a remark, observation, or criticism. **AHLB:** 1288-A (N1) **Strong's:** 4405

697. מֶלַח / מלח / me-lahh **Translation:** Salt **Definition:** An ingredient that adds flavor to food and used in preserving foods. **AHLB:** 2338 (N) **Strong's:** 4417

698. מִלְחָמָה / מלחמה / mil-hha-mah **Translation:** Battle **Definition:** A struggle between two armies. **AHLB:** 2305 (h1) **Strong's:** 4421

699. מֶלֶךְ / מלך / me-lekh **Translation:** King **Definition:** The male ruler of a nation or city state. **AHLB:** 2340 (N) **Strong's:** 4428

700. מַלְכָּה / מלכה / mal-kah **Translation:** Queen **Definition:** A female ruler of a region. **AHLB:** 2340 (N1) **Strong's:** 4436

701. מַלְכוּת / מלכות / mal-kut **Translation:** Empire **Definition:** The area under the control of a king. **AHLB:** 2340 (N3) **Strong's:** 4438

702. מַמְלָכָה / ממלכה / mam-la-khah **Translation:** Kingdom **Definition:** The area under the control of a king. **AHLB:** 2340 (a1) **Strong's:** 4467

703. מְנוֹרָה / מנורה / m-no-rah **Translation:** Lampstand **Definition:** A platform, sometimes elevated, for holding a lamp. **AHLB:** 1319-J (k1) **Strong's:** 4501

704. מִנְחָה / מנחה / min-hhah **Translation:** Donation **Definition:** The act of making a gift or a free contribution.

What is brought to another as a gift. **AHLB:** 1307-A (h1) **Strong's:** 4503

705. מָסָךְ / 𐤌𐤎𐤊 / ma-sak **Translation:** Canopy **Definition:** The covering of a temporary shelter. **AHLB:** 1333-A (a) **Strong's:** 4539

706. מַסֵּכָה / 𐤌𐤉𐤎𐤊𐤄 / ma-sey-khah **Translation:** Cast image **Definition:** A molten metal that is poured in a cast to form images. **AHLB:** 2412 (a1) **Strong's:** 4541

707. מְסִלָּה / 𐤌𐤎𐤉𐤋𐤄 / m-si-lah **Translation:** Highway **Definition:** A road constructed above the surrounding area. **AHLB:** 1334-M (k1) **Strong's:** 4546

708. מִסְפָּר / 𐤌𐤎𐤐𐤓 / mis-phar **Translation:** Number **Definition:** A sum of units. Counting as a recording. **AHLB:** 2500 (h) **Strong's:** 4557

709. מֵעָה / 𐤌𐤏𐤄 / mey-ah **Translation:** Abdomen **Definition:** The gut, the internal organs of the lower torso, the seat of the unconscious mind. **AHLB:** 1292-H (N) **Strong's:** 4578

710. מָעוֹז / 𐤌𐤏𐤅𐤆 / ma-oz **Translation:** Stronghold **Definition:** A place of strength and refuge such as a mountain, fortress or rock. **AHLB:** 1352-J (a) **Strong's:** 4581

711. מְעַט / 𐤌𐤏𐤈 / m-at **Translation:** Small amount **Definition:** Something that is few or small in size or amount. **AHLB:** 2347 (N) **Strong's:** 4592

712. מְעִיל / / m-il **Translation:** Cloak **Definition:** A loose outer garment worn over other clothes both by men and women. **AHLB:** 1357-M (k) **Strong's:** 4598

713. מַעַל / / ma-al **Translation:** Transgression **Definition:** An unintentional or treacherous act that results in error. **AHLB:** 2349 (N) **Strong's:** 4604

714. מַעַל / / ma-al **Translation:** Upward **Definition:** In a direction from lower to higher. **AHLB:** 1357-A (a) **Strong's:** 4605

715. מַעֲלָה / / ma-a-lah **Translation:** Step **Definition:** A straight or stepped incline for ascending and descending. **AHLB:** 1357-A (a1) **Strong's:** 4609

716. מַעֲלָל / / ma-a-lal **Translation:** Works **Definition:** What is done or performed. **AHLB:** 1357-B (a) **Strong's:** 4611

717. מְעָרָה / / m-a-rah **Translation:** Cave **Definition:** A natural underground chamber or series of chambers that open to the surface. A hole in the rock. **AHLB:** 1250-A (k1) **Strong's:** 4631

718. מַעֲשֶׂה / / ma-a-seh **Translation:** Work **Definition:** Activity where one exerts strength or faculties to do or perform something. An action. **AHLB:** 1360-H (a) **Strong's:** 4639

719. מַעֲשֵׂר / / ma-a-seyr **Translation:** Tenth part **Definition:** One portion of a whole divided into ten equal portions. **AHLB:** 2563 (a) **Strong's:** 4643

720. מַצֵּבָה / / ma-tsey-vah **Translation:** Monument **Definition:** A lasting evidence, reminder, or example of someone or something. As standing tall and firm. **AHLB:** 2426 (a1) **Strong's:** 4676

721. מַצָּה / / mats-tsah **Translation:** Unleavened bread **Definition:** A hard and flat bread or cake made without yeast. **AHLB:** 1294-B (N1) **Strong's:** 4682

722. מִצְוָה / / mits-wah **Translation:** Directive **Definition:** Serving or intended to guide, govern, or influence; serving to point direction. **AHLB:** 1397-H (h1) **Strong's:** 4687

More about the word מִצְוָה

The word command, as well as commandment, are used to translate the Hebrew word mits'vah but does not properly convey the meaning of mits'vah. The word command implies words of force or power as a General commands his troops. The word mits'vah is better understood as a directive. To see the picture painted by this word, it is helpful to look at a related word, tsiyon (which is also the name Zion) meaning a desert or a landmark. The Ancient Hebrews were a nomadic people who traveled the deserts in search of green pastures for their flocks. A nomad uses the various rivers, mountains, rock outcroppings, etc as landmarks to give them their direction. The verbal root of mits'vah and tsiyon is tsavah meaning to direct one on a journey. The mits'vah of the Bible are not commands, or rules and regulations, they are directives or landmarks that we look for to guide us.

723. מִקְדָּשׁ / 𐤌𐤒𐤃𐤔 / miq-dash **Translation:** Sanctuary **Definition:** A place set apart for a special purpose. **AHLB:** 2700 (h) **Strong's:** 4720

724. מָקוֹם / 𐤌𐤒𐤅𐤌 / ma-qom **Translation:** Area **Definition:** An indefinite region or expanse; a particular part of a surface or body. **AHLB:** 1427-J (a) **Strong's:** 4725

725. מִקְנֶה / 𐤌𐤒𐤍𐤄 / miq-neh **Translation:** Livestock **Definition:** Animals kept or raised for use or pleasure. What is purchased or possessed. **AHLB:** 1428-H (h) **Strong's:** 4735

726. מַר / 𐤌𐤓 / mar **Translation:** Bitter **Definition:** A difficult taste or experience. **AHLB:** 1296-A (N) **Strong's:** 4751

727. מַרְאֶה / 𐤌𐤓𐤀𐤄 / mar-eh **Translation:** Appearance **Definition:** What is seen or is in sight. **AHLB:** 1438-H (a) **Strong's:** 4758

728. מָרוֹם / 𐤌𐤓𐤅𐤌 / ma-rom **Translation:** Heights **Definition:** A place of considerable or great elevation. **AHLB:** 1450-J (a) **Strong's:** 4791

729. מֶרְכָּבָה / 𐤌𐤓𐤊𐤁𐤄 / mer-ka-vah **Translation:** Chariot **Definition:** A two-wheeled horse-drawn battle car of ancient times used also in processions and races. **AHLB:** 2769 (k1) **Strong's:** 4818

730. מִרְמָה / 𐤌𐤓𐤌𐤄 / mir-mah **Translation:** Deceit **Definition:** The act or practice of not being honest. **AHLB:** 1450-A (h1) **Strong's:** 4820

731. מָשְׁחָה / / mash-hhah **Translation:** Ointment **Definition:** An oil or other liquid that is smeared on an animal or person for healing or dedication. **AHLB:** 2357 (N^1) **Strong's:** 4888

732. מָשִׁיחַ / / ma-shi-ahh **Translation:** Smeared **Definition:** Someone or something that has been smeared with an oil as a medication or a sign of taking an office. **AHLB:** 2357 (b) **Strong's:** 4899

More about the word מָשִׁיחַ

The word Messiah is a transliteration of the Hebrew word meshiahh. This word comes from the root mashahh meaning "to smear" as in Jeremiah 22:14 where it is usually translated as "painted". In the ancient world olive oil was a very versatile commodity. It was used in cooking and because of its disinfectant quality, it was used as a medicine. No shepherd was without a flask of olive oil, which he smeared on himself, or his sheep's injuries. The verb mashahh is also translated as "anointed", as in Exodus 29:7, in the sense of smearing olive oil on the head. This ceremony was performed on anyone becoming a king, priest or prophet in the service of YHWH. The noun meshiahh literally means, "One who is smeared with oil for an office of authority." This word is also used for any "one who holds an office of authority" even if that person was not literally smeared with oil. A good example of this is Cyrus, the King of Persia. While he was not ceremonially smeared with oil, he was one of authority who served Yahweh through his decree allowing Israel to return to Jerusalem.

733. מִשְׁכָּב / / mish-kav **Translation:** Laying place **Definition:** The location one lays for rest or sleep. **AHLB:** 2834 (h) **Strong's:** 4904

734. מִשְׁכָּן / / mish-kan **Translation:** Dwelling **Definition:** A place of habitation or residence. **AHLB:** 2838 (h) **Strong's:** 4908

735. מָשָׁל / / ma-shal **Translation:** Comparison **Definition:** An illustration of similitude. Often a parable or proverb as a story of comparisons. **AHLB:** 2359 (N) **Strong's:** 4912

736. מִשְׁמֶרֶת / / mish-me-ret **Translation:** Charge **Definition:** A person or thing committed to the care of another. What is given to be watched over and protected. **AHLB:** 2853 (h2) **Strong's:** 4931

737. מִשְׁנֶה / / mish-neh **Translation:** Double **Definition:** To make twice as great or as many. As a second or a multiple of two. **AHLB:** 1474-H (h) **Strong's:** 4932

738. מִשְׁפָּחָה / / mish-pa-hhah **Translation:** Family **Definition:** A group of persons of common ancestry. A group of people joined together by certain convictions or common affiliation. **AHLB:** 2863 (h1) **Strong's:** 4940

739. מִשְׁפָּט / / mish-pat **Translation:** Decision **Definition:** A pronounced opinion. **AHLB:** 2864 (h) **Strong's:** 4941

740. מִשְׁקָל / / mish-qal **Translation:** Weight **Definition:** The amount a thing weighs. Relative heaviness. **AHLB:** 2874 (h) **Strong's:** 4948

741. מִשְׁתֶּה / / mish-teh **Translation:** Banquet **Definition:** An elaborate meal often accompanied by a ceremony. **AHLB:** 1482-H (h) **Strong's:** 4960

742. מָתֶן / / ma-ten **Translation:** Waist **Definition:** The slender part of the body above the hips. **AHLB:** 2363 (N) **Strong's:** 4975

Nun

743. נְאֻם / / n-um **Translation:** Utterance **Definition:** An oral or written statement. **AHLB:** 1312-D (N) **Strong's:** 5002

744. נָבִיא / / na-vi **Translation:** Prophet **Definition:** One who utters the words or instructions of Elohiym that are received through a vision or dream. **AHLB:** 1301-E (b) **Strong's:** 5030

745. נֶבֶל / / ne-vel **Translation:** Pitcher **Definition:** A vessel for holding liquids such as a bottle or skin bag. Also a musical instrument of similar shape. **AHLB:** 2369 (N) **Strong's:** 5035

746. נְבֵלָה / / n-vey-lah **Translation:** Carcass **Definition:** The remains of a dead creature or person. **AHLB:** 2369 (N1) **Strong's:** 5038

747. נֶגֶב / / ne-gev **Translation:** South side **Definition:** An area of land or a section that is to the south. **AHLB:** 2371 (N) **Strong's:** 5045

748. נָגִיד / / na-gid **Translation:** Noble **Definition:** One who rules or is in charge of others through instructions. **AHLB:** 2372 (b) **Strong's:** 5057

749. נֶגַע / / ne-ga **Translation:** Plague **Definition:** An epidemic disease causing high mortality. An epidemic or other sore or illness as a touch from Elohiym. **AHLB:** 2376 (N) **Strong's:** 5061

750. נְדָבָה / / n-da-vah **Translation:** Freewill offering **Definition:** A voluntary or spontaneous gift as an offering out of respect or devotion. **AHLB:** 2380 (N^{1}) **Strong's:** 5071

751. נִדָּה / / ni-dah **Translation:** Removal **Definition:** Something that is taken away or thrown out. A menstruating woman that is removed from the camp. **AHLB:** 1303-M (N1) **Strong's:** 5079

752. נָדִיב / / na-div **Translation:** Willing **Definition:** To give honor or offering out of one's own free will. **AHLB:** 2380 (b) **Strong's:** 5081

753. נֶדֶר / / ne-der **Translation:** Vow **Definition:** To promise solemnly. **AHLB:** 2385 (N) **Strong's:** 5088

754. נָהָר / 𐤍𐤄𐤓 / na-har **Translation:** River **Definition:** A natural stream of water of considerable volume. The life-giving water that washes over the soil. **AHLB:** 1319-G (N) **Strong's:** 5104

755. נָוֶה / 𐤍𐤅𐤄 / na-weh **Translation:** Abode **Definition:** The dwelling place of man (home), Elohiym (mountain) or animal (pasture or stable). **AHLB:** 1305-J (N) **Strong's:** 5116

756. נֶזֶר / 𐤍𐤆𐤓 / ne-zer **Translation:** Crown **Definition:** An object showing Kingship or authority. Also, a sign upon the head as a sign of dedication. **AHLB:** 2390 (N) **Strong's:** 5145

757. נִחוֹחַ / 𐤍𐤉𐤇𐤅𐤇 / ni-hho-ahh **Translation:** Sweet **Definition:** Pleasing to the taste. Not sour, bitter or salty. Something that smells pleasing. **AHLB:** 1310-B (bc) **Strong's:** 5207

758. נַחַל / 𐤍𐤇𐤋 / na-hhal **Translation:** Wadi **Definition:** The bed or valley of a stream. A choice piece of land desired in an inheritance because of its fertility. **AHLB:** 2391 (N) **Strong's:** 5158

759. נַחֲלָה / 𐤍𐤇𐤋𐤄 / na-hha-lah **Translation:** Inheritance **Definition:** The acquisition of a possession from past generations. **AHLB:** 2391 (N1) **Strong's:** 5159

760. נָחָשׁ / 𐤍𐤇𐤔 / na-hhash **Translation:** Serpent **Definition:** A poisonous snake that hisses, creeps and bites. **AHLB:** 2395 (N) **Strong's:** 5175

761. נְחֹשֶׁת / 𐤍𐤇𐤅𐤔𐤕 / n-hho-shet **Translation:** Copper **Definition:** A malleable, ductile, metallic element having a characteristic reddish-brown color. A precious metal. **AHLB:** 2395 (c2) **Strong's:** 5178

762. נֵכָר / 𐤍𐤊𐤓 / ney-khar **Translation:** Foreigner **Definition:** A person belonging to or owing allegiance to a foreign country. **AHLB:** 2406 (N) **Strong's:** 5236

763. נָכְרִי / 𐤍𐤊𐤓𐤉 / nakh-ri **Translation:** Foreign **Definition:** Situated outside one's own country. Alien in character. A strange person, place or thing as being unrecognized. **AHLB:** 2406 (f) **Strong's:** 5237

764. נֶסֶךְ / 𐤍𐤎𐤊 / ne-sek **Translation:** Pouring **Definition:** A liquid poured out as an offering or the pouring of a molten metal to form images. **AHLB:** 2412 (N) **Strong's:** 5262

765. נָעוּר / 𐤍𐤏𐤅𐤓 / na-ur **Translation:** Young age **Definition:** A person of short life. **AHLB:** 2418 (d) **Strong's:** 5271

766. נַעַר / 𐤍𐤏𐤓 / na-ar **Translation:** Young man **Definition:** A male that has moved from youth to young adulthood. **AHLB:** 2418 (N) **Strong's:** 5288

767. נַעֲרָה / 𐤍𐤏𐤓𐤄 / na-a-rah **Translation:** Young woman **Definition:** A female that has moved from youth to young adulthood. **AHLB:** 2418 (N1) **Strong's:** 5291

768. נֶפֶשׁ / 𐤍𐤐𐤔 / ne-phesh **Translation:** Being **Definition:** The whole of a person, god or creature including the body, mind, emotion, character and inner parts. **AHLB:** 2424 (N) **Strong's:** 5315

769. נֶצַח / / ne-tsahh **Translation:** Continually **Definition:** Happening without interruption or cessation; continuous in time. **AHLB:** 2427 (N) **Strong's:** 5331

770. נָקִי / / na-qi **Translation:** Innocent **Definition:** Free from guilt or sin. A state of innocence as an infant. **AHLB:** 1318-A (f) **Strong's:** 5355

771. נְקָמָה / / n-qa-mah **Translation:** Vengeance **Definition:** The desire for revenge. **AHLB:** 2433 (N^1) **Strong's:** 5360

772. נֵר / / neyr **Translation:** Lamp **Definition:** A container for an inflammable liquid, as oil, which is burned at a wick as a means of illumination. **AHLB:** 1319-A (N) **Strong's:** 5216

773. נָשִׂיא / / na-si **Translation:** Captain **Definition:** A military leader; the commander of a unit or a body of troops. The leader of a family, tribe or people as one who carries the burdens of the people. **AHLB:** 1314-E (b) **Strong's:** 5387

774. נָתִיב / / na-tiv **Translation:** Path **Definition:** A trail or road used by travelers. **AHLB:** 2448 (b^1) **Strong's:** 5410

Samehh

775. סָבִיב / / sa-viv **Translation:** All around **Definition:** On all sides; enclose so as to surround; in rotation or succession. A circling or bordering about the edge. **AHLB:** 1324-B (b1) **Strong's:** 5439

776. סוּס / 𐤎𐤅𐤎 / sus **Translation:** Horse **Definition:** A domesticated animal used as a beast of burden, a draft animal or for riding. **AHLB:** 1337-J (N) **Strong's:** 5483

777. סוּף / 𐤐𐤅𐤎 / suph **Translation:** Reeds **Definition:** The plants that grow at the edge, or lip, of a river or pond. This word can also mean the edge or conclusion of something. **AHLB:** 1339-J (N) **Strong's:** 5488

778. סִיר / 𐤓𐤉𐤎 / sir **Translation:** Pot **Definition:** A vessel used for cooking or storing. **AHLB:** 1342-M (N) **Strong's:** 5518

779. סֻכָּה / 𐤄𐤊𐤅𐤎 / su-kah **Translation:** Booth **Definition:** A temporary shelter; a small enclosure; dwelling place. **AHLB:** 1333-J (N1) **Strong's:** 5521

780. סֶלָה / 𐤄𐤋𐤎 / se-lah **Translation:** Selah **Definition:** A musical term, possibly a lifting of the sound. **AHLB:** 1334-H (N) **Strong's:** 5542

781. סֶלַע / 𐤏𐤋𐤎 / se-la **Translation:** Cliff **Definition:** A high rock, cliff or towering rock, as a place of defense. **AHLB:** 2484 (N) **Strong's:** 5553

782. סֹלֶת / 𐤕𐤋𐤅𐤎 / so-let **Translation:** Flour **Definition:** Finely ground meal of grain used for making bread. **AHLB:** 1334-J (N2) **Strong's:** 5560

783. סַף / 𐤐𐤎 / saph **Translation:** Tub **Definition:** A container with a lip. The lip of the door. **AHLB:** 1339-A (N) **Strong's:** 5592

784. סֵפֶר / 𐤓𐤐𐤎 / sey-pher **Translation:** Scroll **Definition:** A document or record written on a sheet of papyrus, leather or parchment and rolled up for storage. **AHLB:** 2500 (e1) **Strong's:** 5612

785. סָרִיס / / sa-ris **Translation:** Eunuch **Definition:** A castrated man. As eunuchs were used as officers, may also mean an officer. **AHLB:** 2510 (b) **Strong's:** 5631

786. סֵתֶר / / sey-ter **Translation:** Protection **Definition:** A shelter or other place of hiding. **AHLB:** 2516 (N) **Strong's:** 5643

Ayin

787. עָב / / av **Translation:** Thick **Definition:** Heavily compacted material, such as a cloud, forest or thicket, and is filled with darkness. **AHLB:** 1508-A (N) **Strong's:** 5645

788. עֶבֶד / / e-ved **Translation:** Servant **Definition:** One who provides a service to another, as a slave, bondservant or hired hand. **AHLB:** 2518 (N) **Strong's:** 5650

789. עֲבֹדָה / / a-vo-dah **Translation:** Service **Definition:** Labor provided by a servant or slave. **AHLB:** 2518 (c1) **Strong's:** 5656

790. עֵבֶר / / ey-ver **Translation:** Other side **Definition:** As being across from this side. **AHLB:** 2520 (N) **Strong's:** 5676

791. עֶבְרָה / / ev-rah **Translation:** Wrath **Definition:** Strong vengeful anger. As crossing over from peace. **AHLB:** 2520 (N1) **Strong's:** 5678

792. עֵגֶל / / ey-gel **Translation:** Bullock **Definition:** A young bull. Also, insinuating strength. **AHLB:** 2524 (N) **Strong's:** 5695

793. עֲגָלָה / / a-ga-lah **Translation:** Cart **Definition:** A heavy, two-wheeled vehicle, animal-drawn, used for transporting freight or for farming. **AHLB:** 2524 (N^1) **Strong's:** 5699

794. עֵד / / eyd **Translation:** Witness **Definition:** Attestation of a fact or event. An object, person or group that affords evidence. **AHLB:** 1349-A (N) **Strong's:** 5707

795. עַד / / ad **Translation:** Until **Definition:** The conclusion of a determinate period of time. **AHLB:** 1349-A (N) **Strong's:** 5704

796. עֵדָה / / ey-dah **Translation:** Company **Definition:** A group of persons or things for carrying on a project or undertaking; a group with a common testimony. May also mean a witness or testimony. **AHLB:** 1349-A (N1) **Strong's:** 5712

797. עֵדוּת / / ey-dut **Translation:** Testimony **Definition:** Speaking what you have experienced or witnessed. **AHLB:** 1349-A (N3) **Strong's:** 5715

798. עֵדֶר / / ey-der **Translation:** Drove **Definition:** A group of animals driven or moving in a body. **AHLB:** 2530 (N) **Strong's:** 5739

799. עוֹד / / od **Translation:** Yet again **Definition:** A repeating of something. **AHLB:** 1349-J (N) **Strong's:** 5750

800. עֹולָם / 𐤏𐤅𐤋𐤌 / o-lam **Translation:** Distant time **Definition:** A time in the far past or future, as a time hidden from the present. **AHLB:** 2544 (g) **Strong's:** 5769

More about the word עֹולָם

Hebrew words used for space are also used for time. The Hebrew word qedem means "east" but is also the same word for the "past." The Hebrew word olam literally means "beyond the horizon." When looking off in the far distance it is difficult to make out any details and what is beyond that horizon cannot be seen. This concept is the olam. The word olam is also used for time for the distant past or the distant future as a time that is difficult to know or perceive. This word is frequently translated as "eternity" meaning a continual span of time that never ends. In the Hebrew mind it is simply what is at or beyond the horizon, a very distant time. A common phrase in the Hebrew is "l'olam va'ed" and is usually translated as "forever and ever," but in the Hebrew it means "to the distant horizon and again" meaning "a very distant time and even further."

801. עָוֹן / 𐤍𐤅𐤅𐤏 / a-won **Translation:** Iniquity **Definition:** Gross injustice; wickedness. The result of twisted actions. **AHLB:** 1512-A (m) **Strong's:** 5771

802. עוֹף / 𐤏𐤅𐤐 / oph **Translation:** Flyer **Definition:** A flying creature such as a bird or insect. **AHLB:** 1362-J (N) **Strong's:** 5775

803. עִוֵּר / / i-weyr **Translation:** Blind **Definition:** A darkness of the eye. **AHLB:** 1526-J (N) **Strong's:** 5787

804. עוֹר / / or **Translation:** Skin **Definition:** The integument covering men or animals, as well as leather made from animal skins. The husk of a seed. **AHLB:** 1365-J (N) **Strong's:** 5785

805. עֵז / / eyz **Translation:** She-goat **Definition:** A female goat. **AHLB:** 1513-A (N) **Strong's:** 5795

806. עֹז / / oz **Translation:** Boldness **Definition:** Knowing one's position or authority and standing in it. Strengthened and protected from danger. **AHLB:** 1352-J (N) **Strong's:** 5797

807. עֶזְרָה / / ez-rah **Translation:** Help **Definition:** Providing assistance or relief to another. **AHLB:** 2535 (N^2) **Strong's:** 5833

808. עַיִן / / a-yin **Translation:** Eye **Definition:** The organ of sight or vision that tears when a person weeps. A spring that weeps water out of the ground. **AHLB:** 1359-M (N) **Strong's:** 5869

809. עִיר / / ir **Translation:** City **Definition:** An inhabited place of greater size, population, or importance than a town or village. Usually protected by a wall. **AHLB:** 1526-M (N) **Strong's:** 5892

810. עַל / / al **Translation:** Upon **Definition:** To be on or over in the sense of the yoke that is placed on the neck of the ox. **AHLB:** 1357-A (N) **Strong's:** 5921

811. עֹל / / ol **Translation:** Yoke **Definition:** A wooden bar or frame by which two draft animals are joined at the heads or necks for working together. **AHLB:** 1357-J (N) **Strong's:** 5923

812. עֹלָה / / o-lah **Translation:** Rising **Definition:** A rising of smoke from a burnt offering. Captivity in the sense of placing a yoke on the captives. **AHLB:** 1357-J (N1) **Strong's:** 5930

813. עֶלְיוֹן / / el-yon **Translation:** Upper **Definition:** Higher than the others. **AHLB:** 1357-A (fj) **Strong's:** 5945

814. עַם / / am **Translation:** People **Definition:** A large group of men or women. **AHLB:** 1358-A (N) **Strong's:** 5971

815. עַמוּד / / a-mud **Translation:** Pillar **Definition:** A standing upright post or column. **AHLB:** 2550 (d) **Strong's:** 5982

816. עָמָל / / a-mal **Translation:** Labor **Definition:** To exert one's power of body or mind, especially with painful or strenuous effort. A labor that causes grief, pain or weariness. A laborer as one who toils. **AHLB:** 2551 (N) **Strong's:** 5999

817. עֵמֶק / / ey-meq **Translation:** Valley **Definition:** An elongated depression between ranges of hills or mountains. Also, obscure, in the sense of dark. **AHLB:** 2553 (N) **Strong's:** 6010

818. עָנָו / / a-naw **Translation:** Gentle **Definition:** A trait of being meek or humble. **AHLB:** 1359-K (N) **Strong's:** 6035

819. עֳנִי / a-ni **Translation:** Affliction **Definition:** The cause of persistent suffering, pain or distress. **AHLB:** 1359-A (f) **Strong's:** 6040

820. עָנִי / a-ni **Translation:** Afflicted **Definition:** One who suffers or is in pain or distress. **AHLB:** 1359-A (f) **Strong's:** 6041

821. עֲנָן / a-nan **Translation:** Cloud **Definition:** A visible mass of particles of water or ice in the form of fog, mist, or haze suspended usually at a considerable height in the air. **AHLB:** 1359-B (N) **Strong's:** 6051

822. עָפָר / a-phar **Translation:** Powder **Definition:** Matter in a fine particulate state. An abundant amount of powdery substance as dust or ash. **AHLB:** 2565 (N) **Strong's:** 6083

823. עֵץ / eyts **Translation:** Tree **Definition:** A woody perennial plant with a supporting stem or trunk and multiple branches. Meaning "wood" when written in the plural form. **AHLB:** 1363-A (N) **Strong's:** 6086

824. עֵצָה / ey-tsah **Translation:** Counsel **Definition:** Advice given in the sense of being the firm support of the community. **AHLB:** 1363-A (N1) **Strong's:** 6098

825. עָצוּם / a-tsum **Translation:** Numerous **Definition:** Involving more than one. **AHLB:** 2569 (d) **Strong's:** 6099

826. עֶצֶם / e-tsem **Translation:** Bone **Definition:** The hard tissue of which the skeleton is chiefly composed. As a numerous amount. **AHLB:** 2569 (N) **Strong's:** 6106

827. עֶרֶב / e-rev **Translation:** Evening **Definition:** The latter part and close of the day and the early part of the night. Dark of the evening or dark-skinned people. Also the willow from its dark color. **AHLB:** 2907 (N) **Strong's:** 6153

828. עֲרָבָה / a-ra-vah **Translation:** Desert **Definition:** An expanse of land often barren of vegetation and people. **AHLB:** 2907 (N1) **Strong's:** 6160

829. עֶרְוָה / er-wah **Translation:** Nakedness **Definition:** The state of being without clothing. Idiomatic for sexual relations. **AHLB:** 1365-K (N1) **Strong's:** 6172

830. עֵרֶךְ / ey-rek **Translation:** Arrangement **Definition:** Set in a row or in order according to rank or age. In parallel. Arranged items in juxtaposition. **AHLB:** 2576 (N) **Strong's:** 6187

831. עָרֵל / a-reyl **Translation:** Uncircumcised **Definition:** A male with a foreskin. **AHLB:** 2577 (N) **Strong's:** 6189

832. עֹרֶף / o-reph **Translation:** Neck **Definition:** The part of a person that connects the head with the body. **AHLB:** 2580 (N) **Strong's:** 6203

833. עֵשֶׂב / ey-sev **Translation:** Herb **Definition:** The grasses and plants of the field used for their medicinal, savory, or aromatic qualities. **AHLB:** 2561 (N) **Strong's:** 6212

834. עָשָׁן / / a-shan **Translation:** Smoke **Definition:** The gaseous products of combustion. **AHLB:** 2583 (N) **Strong's:** 6227

835. עֹשֶׁר / / o-ser **Translation:** Riches **Definition:** Wealth. The possessions that make one wealthy. **AHLB:** 2585 (N) **Strong's:** 6239

836. עִשָּׂרוֹן / / i-sa-ron **Translation:** One-tenth **Definition:** An equal part of something divided into ten parts. **AHLB:** 2563 (j) **Strong's:** 6241

837. עֵת / / eyt **Translation:** Appointed time **Definition:** A fixed or officially set event, occasion or date. **AHLB:** 1367-A (N) **Strong's:** 6256

838. עַתּוּד / / a-tud **Translation:** He-goat **Definition:** A male member of a flock of goats. **AHLB:** 2587 (d) **Strong's:** 6260

Pey

839. פֵּאָה / / pey-ah **Translation:** Edge **Definition:** The border or boundary of an object or a region. The thin cutting edge of a blade. **AHLB:** 1369-A (N1) **Strong's:** 6285

840. פֶּה / / peh **Translation:** Mouth **Definition:** The opening through which food enters the body. Any opening. **AHLB:** 1373-A (N) **Strong's:** 6310

841. פַּח / / pahh **Translation:** Wire **Definition:** A slender, string-like piece or filament of relatively rigid or flexible metal often used for snares. **AHLB:** 1376-A (N) **Strong's:** 6341

842. פַּחַד / / pa-hhad **Translation:** Awe **Definition:** As shaking when in the presence of an awesome sight. **AHLB:** 2598 (N) **Strong's:** 6343

843. פֶּחָה / / pe-hhah **Translation:** Governor **Definition:** A ruler or overseer of a people or region. **AHLB:** 1376-H (N) **Strong's:** 6346

844. פִּילֶגֶשׁ / / pi-le-gesh **Translation:** Concubine **Definition:** Cohabitation of persons not legally married; a woman living in a socially recognized state of being a mistress. **AHLB:** 3048 **Strong's:** 6370

845. פְּלֵיטָה / / p-ley-tah **Translation:** Escape **Definition:** To get away, especially from confinement. **AHLB:** 2609 (b1) **Strong's:** 6413

846. פִּנָּה / / pin-nah **Translation:** Corner **Definition:** The point where two lines meet. **AHLB:** 1382-M (N1) **Strong's:** 6438

847. פָּנִים / / pa-nim **Translation:** Face **Definition:** The front part of the human head; outward appearance. One present, in the sense of being in the face of another. Always written in the plural form. **AHLB:** 1382-H (N) **Strong's:** 6440

848. פְּנִימִי / / p-ni-mi **Translation:** Inner **Definition:** What is inside or inward. **AHLB:** 2615 (bf) **Strong's:** 6442

849. פֶּסַח / pe-sahh **Translation:** Passover **Definition:** The day of deliverance from Egypt. Also the feast remembering this day and the lamb that is sacrificed for this feast. **AHLB:** n/a **Strong's:** 6453

850. פֶּסֶל / pe-sel **Translation:** Sculpture **Definition:** A figurine that is formed and shaped from stone, wood or clay. **AHLB:** 2619 (N) **Strong's:** 6459

851. פֹּעַל / po-al **Translation:** Deed **Definition:** A work or action that is made. **AHLB:** 2622 (g) **Strong's:** 6467

852. פַּעַם / pa-am **Translation:** Footstep **Definition:** A stroke of time as a rhythmic beating of time, one moment after the other. A moment in time. A foot or leg in the sense of stepping. **AHLB:** 2623 (N) **Strong's:** 6471

853. פְּקֻדָּה / p-qu-dah **Translation:** Oversight **Definition:** A careful watching over. **AHLB:** 2630 (d1) **Strong's:** 6486

854. פַּר / par **Translation:** Bull **Definition:** A large male un-castrated bovine. **AHLB:** 1388-A (N) **Strong's:** 6499

855. פָּרָה / pa-rah **Translation:** Cow **Definition:** The mature female of cattle. **AHLB:** 1388-A (N^1) **Strong's:** 6510

856. פְּרִי / p-ri **Translation:** Produce **Definition:** Agricultural products, especially fresh fruits and vegetables. The harvested product of a crop. **AHLB:** 1388-H (f) **Strong's:** 6529

857. פָּרֹכֶת / [illegible] / pa-ro-khet **Translation:** Tent curtain **Definition:** A wall of fabric or hung from the roof to make a dividing of a room. **AHLB:** 2638 (c^2) **Strong's:** 6532

858. פָּרָשׁ / [illegible] / pa-rash **Translation:** Horseman **Definition:** One that rides a horse. **AHLB:** 2644 (N) **Strong's:** 6571

859. פֶּשַׁע / [illegible] / pe-sha **Translation:** Transgression **Definition:** The exceeding of due bounds or limits. **AHLB:** 2647 (N) **Strong's:** 6588

860. פֶּתַח / [illegible] / pe-tahh **Translation:** Opening **Definition:** Something that is open, as an entrance or opening of a tent, house or city. **AHLB:** 2649 (N) **Strong's:** 6607

Tsade

861. צֹאן / [illegible] / tson **Translation:** Flocks **Definition:** Groups of birds or animals assembled or herded together. **AHLB:** 1405-J (N) **Strong's:** 6629

862. צָבָא / [illegible] / tsa-va **Translation:** Army **Definition:** A large organized group mustered together and armed for war or service. **AHLB:** 1393-E (N) **Strong's:** 6635

863. צְבִי / [illegible] / ts-vi **Translation:** Gazelle buck **Definition:** Any small antelope species noted for graceful movements. **AHLB:** 1393-A (f) **Strong's:** 6643

864. צַד / [illegible] / tsad **Translation:** Side **Definition:** An area next to something. **AHLB:** 1395-A (N) **Strong's:** 6654

865. צַדִּיק / צדיק / tsa-diq **Translation:** Correct **Definition:** To make or set right. Conforming to fact, standard or truth. **AHLB:** 2658 (b) **Strong's:** 6662

More about the word צַדִּיק

This word is often translated as "righteous," an abstract word. In order to understand this word from an Hebraic mindset, we must uncover its original concrete meaning. One of the best ways to determine the original concrete meaning of a word is to find it being used in a sentence where its concrete meaning can be seen. The problem with the word tsadiyq, and its verb form tsadaq, is that there are no uses of this word in its concrete meaning. The next method is to compare how the word in question is paralleled with other Hebrew words as commonly found in the poetical passages of the Bible. Sometimes these parallels will be synonyms and other times antonyms. When we look at the word tsadiyq we find that it is commonly paralleled with the word "rasha". Rasha is usually translated as "wicked" but has a concrete meaning of "to depart from the path and become lost". From this we can conclude that a tsadiyq is one who remains on the path. The path is the course through life which Elohiym has outlined for us in his word.

866. צֶדֶק / / tse-deq **Translation:** Corrected **Definition:** The following of the established path or course of action. **AHLB:** 2658 (N) **Strong's:** 6664

867. צְדָקָה / / ts-da-qah **Translation:** Correctness **Definition:** Conformity to fact, standard or truth. **AHLB:** 2658 (N1) **Strong's:** 6666

868. צַוָּאר / / tsa-war **Translation:** Back of the neck **Definition:** The nape between the shoulders and the head. **AHLB:** 1411-D (g) **Strong's:** 6677

869. צוֹם / / tsom **Translation:** Fast **Definition:** A purposeful abstinence from food. **AHLB:** 1404-J (N) **Strong's:** 6685

870. צֵל / / tseyl **Translation:** Shadow **Definition:** The dark figure cast on a surface by a body intercepting the rays from a light source. **AHLB:** 1403-A (N) **Strong's:** 6738

871. צֵלָע / / tsey-la **Translation:** Rib **Definition:** Any of the paired bony or cartilaginous bones that stiffen the walls of the thorax and protect the organs beneath. A ridge of a hill from its similar shape to a rib. Also, the side. **AHLB:** 2664 (N) **Strong's:** 6763

872. צָפוֹן / / tsa-phon **Translation:** North **Definition:** From the North Star which is watched for direction. **AHLB:** 1408-A (j) **Strong's:** 6828

873. צִפּוֹר / / tsi-por **Translation:** Bird **Definition:** A creature distinguished by a body covering of feathers and wings as forelimbs. **AHLB:** 2685 (c) **Strong's:** 6833

874. צַר / / tsar **Translation:** Narrow **Definition:** Of slender width. A narrow, tight place or situation. An enemy or adversary as one who closes in with pressure. **AHLB:** 1411-A (N) **Strong's:** 6862

875. צָרָה / / tsa-rah **Translation:** Trouble **Definition:** To agitate mentally or spiritually; worry; disturb. **AHLB:** 1411-A (N1) **Strong's:** 6869

876. צָרַעַת / / tsa-ra-at **Translation:** Infection **Definition:** A contaminated substance, such as a disease, mold or mildew, on the skin, cloth or a building. **AHLB:** 2691 (N2) **Strong's:** 6883

Quph

877. קֶבֶר / / qe-ver **Translation:** Grave **Definition:** An excavation for the burial of a body. **AHLB:** 2696 (N) **Strong's:** 6913

878. קָדוֹשׁ / / qa-dosh **Translation:** Unique **Definition:** Someone or something that has, or has been given the quality of specialness, and has been separated from the rest for a special purpose. **AHLB:** 2700 (c) **Strong's:** 6918

More about the word קָדוֹשׁ

This word is frequently translated as "holy," another abstract word. When we use the word holy, as in a holy person, we usually associate this with a righteous or pious person. If we use this concept when interpreting the word holy in the

Hebrew Bible, then we are misreading the text, as this is not the meaning of the Hebrew word qadosh. Qadosh literally means "to be set apart for a special purpose". A related word, qedesh, is one who is also set apart for a special purpose but not in the same way we think of "holy," but is a prostitute (Deut 23:17). Israel was qadosh because they were separated from the other nations as servants of Elohiym. The furnishings in the tabernacle were also qadosh, as they were not to be used for anything except for the work in the tabernacle. While we may not think of ourselves as "holy," we are in fact set apart from the world to be Elohiym's servants and his representatives.

879. קָדִים / / qa-dim **Translation:** East wind **Definition:** The wind that comes from the east. Toward the east as the origin of the east wind. **AHLB:** 2698 (b) **Strong's:** 6921

880. קֶדֶם / / qe-dem **Translation:** East **Definition:** The general direction of sunrise. As in front when facing the rising sun. Also, the ancient past. **AHLB:** 2698 (N) **Strong's:** 6924

881. קֹדֶשׁ / / qo-desh **Translation:** Special **Definition:** Someone or something that has the quality of being special; Separated from the rest for a special purpose. **AHLB:** 2700 (g) **Strong's:** 6944

882. קָהָל / 𐤒𐤄𐤋 / qa-hal **Translation:** Assembly **Definition:** A large group, as a gathering of the flock of sheep to the shepherd. **AHLB:** 1426-G (N) **Strong's:** 6951

883. קוֹל / 𐤒𐤅𐤋 / qol **Translation:** Voice **Definition:** The faculty of utterance. Sound of a person, musical instrument, the wind, thunder, etc. **AHLB:** 1426-J (N) **Strong's:** 6963

884. קוֹמָה / 𐤒𐤅𐤌𐤄 / qo-mah **Translation:** Height **Definition:** The highest part or most advanced point; the condition of being tall or high. In the sense of being raised up. **AHLB:** 1427-J (N1) **Strong's:** 6967

885. קָטָן / 𐤒𐤈𐤍 / qa-tan **Translation:** Small **Definition:** Someone or something that is not very large in size, importance, age or significance. **AHLB:** 2703 (N) **Strong's:** 6996

886. קְטֹרֶת / 𐤒𐤈𐤅𐤓𐤕 / q-to-ret **Translation:** Incense **Definition:** Usually made of several spices and or fruits, etc. to emit a fragrance. Used at the altar as a sweet savor. **AHLB:** 2705 (c2) **Strong's:** 7004

887. קְלָלָה / 𐤒𐤋𐤋𐤄 / q-la-lah **Translation:** Annoyance **Definition:** The act of disturbing or irritating. Something that is light in stature; considered worthless as compared with something of much greater value or importance. **AHLB:** 1426-B (N1) **Strong's:** 7045

888. קִנְאָה / 𐤒𐤍𐤀𐤄 / qin-ah **Translation:** Zealousy **Definition:** A protective or suspicious nature. **AHLB:** 1428-E (N1) **Strong's:** 7068

889. קָנֶה / / qa-neh **Translation:** Stalk **Definition:** The main stem and support of a plant. **AHLB:** 1428-H (N) **Strong's:** 7070

890. קֵץ / / qeyts **Translation:** Conclusion **Definition:** To come to an end. The end of a time period or place or the end of something. The border of a country as its edges. **AHLB:** 1432-A (N) **Strong's:** 7093

891. קָצֶה / / qa-tseh **Translation:** Far end **Definition:** The most distant extremity of something; the end or edge. **AHLB:** 1432-H (N) **Strong's:** 7097

892. קָצָה / / qa-tsah **Translation:** Extremity **Definition:** The far end or border of something. The end, corner or edge. **AHLB:** 1432-A (N1) **Strong's:** 7098

893. קָצִיר / / qa-tsir **Translation:** Harvest **Definition:** The season for gathering agricultural crops. Time when the plants are severed from their roots to be used for seed or food. **AHLB:** 2727 (b) **Strong's:** 7105

894. קֶצֶף / / qe-tseph **Translation:** Splinter **Definition:** The sharp flying objects from a snapped piece of wood. Also wrath as flying splinters. **AHLB:** 2726 (N) **Strong's:** 7110

895. קֶרֶב / / qe-rev **Translation:** Within **Definition:** In the sense of being close or in the interior of. An approaching. **AHLB:** 2729 (N) **Strong's:** 7130

896. קֹרְבָּן / / kor-ban **Translation:** Offering **Definition:** Something given to another in devotion. **AHLB:** 2729 (gm) **Strong's:** 7133

897. קָרוֹב / / qa-rov **Translation:** Near **Definition:** Close to; at or within a short distance from. Also, a kin, as a near relative. **AHLB:** 2729 (c) **Strong's:** 7138

898. קִרְיָה / / qir-yah **Translation:** City **Definition:** A large populace of people; a town or village. **AHLB:** 1434-H (f1) **Strong's:** 7151

899. קֶרֶן / / qe-ren **Translation:** Horn **Definition:** One of a pair of bony processes that arise from the head of many animals, sometimes used as a wind instrument. The horn-shaped protrusions of the altar or a musical instrument. **AHLB:** 2732 (N) **Strong's:** 7161

900. קֶרֶשׁ / / qe-resh **Translation:** Board **Definition:** A plank of wood often used to wall off an area or restrict access. **AHLB:** 2736 (N) **Strong's:** 7175

901. קָשֶׁה / / qa-sheh **Translation:** Hard **Definition:** Not easily penetrated; resistant to stress; firm; lacking in responsiveness. **AHLB:** 1435-H (N) **Strong's:** 7186

902. קֶשֶׁת / / qe-shet **Translation:** Bow **Definition:** A weapon made from a stiff branch to shoots arrows. A bow-shaped object such as a rainbow. **AHLB:** 1435-A (N2) **Strong's:** 7198

Resh

903. רֹאשׁ / / rosh **Translation:** Head **Definition:** The top of the body. A person in authority or role of leader. The top, beginning or first of something. **AHLB:** 1458-D (N) **Strong's:** 7218

904. רֵאשִׁית / 𐤓𐤀𐤔𐤉𐤕 / rey-shit **Translation:** Summit **Definition:** The head, top or beginning of a place, such as a river or mountain, or a time, such as an event. The point at which something starts; origin, source. **AHLB:** 1458-D (N4) **Strong's:** 7225

905. רַב / 𐤓𐤁 / rav **Translation:** Abundant **Definition:** Great plenty or supply of numbers (many) or strength (great). One who is abundant in authority such as a master or teacher. Also, an archer as one abundant with arrows. **AHLB:** 1439-A (N) **Strong's:** 7227

906. רֹב / 𐤓𐤅𐤁 / rov **Translation:** Abundance **Definition:** An ample quantity of number (many) or plentiful supply of strength (great). **AHLB:** 1439-J (N) **Strong's:** 7230

907. רֶגֶל / 𐤓𐤂𐤋 / re-gel **Translation:** Foot **Definition:** The terminal part of the leg upon which the human, animal or object stands. **AHLB:** 2749 (N) **Strong's:** 7272

908. רוּחַ / 𐤓𐤅𐤇 / ru-ahh **Translation:** Wind **Definition:** A natural movement of air; breath. The wind of man, animal or Elohiym. The breath. A space in between. **AHLB:** 1445-J (N) **Strong's:** 7307

More about the word רוּחַ

The Hebrew word ru'ach literally means the wind and is derived from the parent root rach meaning a prescribed path. The word rach is not found in the Biblical text but defined by the various child roots derived from it. The child roots derived from this parent root are arach, rachah and yarach. Arach is a traveler, one who follows a prescribed path from one place to another. Rachah is a millstone, which goes round and round in the sense of following a prescribed path to crush grain into flour. Yarach is the root of yere'ach meaning the moon, which follows a prescribed path in the night sky. The child root ru'ach is literally the wind that follows a prescribed path each season. By extension ru'ach means the wind of a man or what is usually translated as spirit. A man's wind is not just a spiritual entity within a man but is understood by the Ancient Hebrews as his character.

909. רֹחַב / / ro-hhav **Translation:** Width **Definition:** Largeness of extent or scope. From the width of a road. **AHLB:** 2759 (g) **Strong's:** 7341

910. רְחוֹב / / r-hhov **Translation:** Street **Definition:** A thoroughfare, especially in a city, town or village. **AHLB:** 2759 (c) **Strong's:** 7339

911. רָחוֹק / / ra-hhoq **Translation:** Distance **Definition:** Separation in space or time. A distant place or time. **AHLB:** 2765 (c) **Strong's:** 7350

912. רַחַם / / ra-hham **Translation:** Bowels **Definition:** The large intestines as encompassed about by the torso. Compassion as coming from the bowels. **AHLB:** 2762 (N) **Strong's:** 7356

913. רִיב / / riv **Translation:** Dispute **Definition:** Bitter, sometimes violent conflict or dissension. **AHLB:** 1439-M (N) **Strong's:** 7379

914. רֵיחַ / / rey-ahh **Translation:** Aroma **Definition:** A distinctive pervasive and usually pleasant or savory smell or odor. **AHLB:** 1445-M (N) **Strong's:** 7381

915. רֶכֶב / / re-khev **Translation:** Chariot **Definition:** A light, two-wheeled battle vehicle for one or two persons, usually drawn by two horses and driven from a standing position. Also, the top millstone as supported on top of the bottom millstone. **AHLB:** 2769 (N) **Strong's:** 7393

916. רְכוּשׁ / / r-khush **Translation:** Goods **Definition:** Something that has economic utility or satisfies an economic want; personal property having intrinsic value but usually excluding money, securities and negotiable instruments. **AHLB:** 2772 (d) **Strong's:** 7399

917. רִמּוֹן / / ri-mon **Translation:** Pomegranate **Definition:** A sweet deep red fruit prolific with seeds. A symbol of compassion and love. **AHLB:** 1450-A (j) **Strong's:** 7416

918. רִנָּה / / ri-nah **Translation:** Shouting **Definition:** A loud exclamation of triumph or joy. **AHLB:** 1451-M (N1) **Strong's:** 7440

919. רֵעַ / / rey-a **Translation:** Companion **Definition:** One that accompanies another. As a close companion. **AHLB:** 1453-A (N) **Strong's:** 7453

920. רָע / 𐤓𐤏 / ra **Translation:** Dysfunctional **Definition:** Impaired or abnormal action other than that for which a person or thing is intended. Something that does not function within its intended purpose. **AHLB:** 1460-A (N) **Strong's:** 7451

921. רָעָב / 𐤓𐤏𐤁 / ra-av **Translation:** Hunger **Definition:** A craving or urgent need for food. **AHLB:** 2777 (N) **Strong's:** 7458

922. רָצוֹן / 𐤓𐤑𐤅𐤍 / ra-tson **Translation:** Will **Definition:** Used to express determination, insistence, persistence, or willfulness. One's desire. **AHLB:** 1455-H (j) **Strong's:** 7522

923. רֶשַׁע / 𐤓𐤔𐤏 / re-sha **Translation:** Lost **Definition:** Departed from the correct path or way. **AHLB:** 2799 (N) **Strong's:** 7562

924. רָשָׁע / 𐤓𐤔𐤏 / ra-sha **Translation:** Lost one **Definition:** One who has departed from the correct path or way. **AHLB:** 2799 (N) **Strong's:** 7563

Shin

925. שְׁאוֹל / 𐤔𐤀𐤅𐤋 / sh-ol **Translation:** Underworld **Definition:** The place of the dead. **AHLB:** 1472-D (c) **Strong's:** 7585

More about the word שְׁאוֹל

The word she'ol was understood as the place where one goes when they die. Was this simply the grave one is buried in, or a place one goes too after they die? This is a difficult question to answer as the Hebrew Bible never really defines she'ol. There is evidence however that they understood it to be more than just the grave. First, the word qever is the normal Hebrew word for a grave and therefore, it is possible that she'ol was understood as something other than the grave. Second, most scriptures using the word she'ol imply a place other than the grave. An example can be found in Genesis 37:35 where Jacob says "I will go down to my son in she'ol." In this account Jacob believed his son Joseph had been eaten by a wild beast and could therefore not be in a grave, yet Jacob knew that he would be with him somewhere-she'ol. The Ancient Hebrews did not know where, or even what, she'ol was. To them it was an unknown place hence. The word she'ol literally means "unknown." It should also be noted that the Ancient Hebrews never speculated on something unknown, it was simply not known and left at that. It is only the Greek mind that desires to know the unknown. It is our Greco-Roman western mindset that needs to know where and what she'ol is.

926. שְׁאֵרִית / [illegible] / sh-ey-rit **Translation:** Remnant **Definition:** A usually small part, member, or trace remaining. **AHLB:** 1480-D (N4) **Strong's:** 7611

927. שְׁבוּעָה / [illegible] / sh-vu-ah **Translation:** Swearing **Definition:** The act of taking an oath. **AHLB:** 2808 (d1) **Strong's:** 7621

928. שְׁבוּת / [illegible] / sh-vut **Translation:** Captivity **Definition:** The state or period of being held, imprisoned, enslaved, or confined. **AHLB:** 1462-H (N3) **Strong's:** 7622

929. שֵׁבֶט / [illegible] / shey-vet **Translation:** Staff **Definition:** A walking stick made from the branch of a tree. Also, a tribe as a branch of the family. **AHLB:** 2805 (N) **Strong's:** 7626

930. שְׁבִי / [illegible] / sh-vi **Translation:** Captive **Definition:** A person who is enslaved or dominated. **AHLB:** 1462-H (f) **Strong's:** 7628

931. שֶׁבֶר / [illegible] / she-ver **Translation:** Shattering **Definition:** Suddenly broken or burst into pieces, as with a violent blow. **AHLB:** 2811 (N) **Strong's:** 7667

932. שַׁבָּת / [illegible] / sha-bat **Translation:** Ceasing **Definition:** A stopping of work or activity; An activity curtailed before completion. The seventh day of the week (often translated as Sabbath) when all business ceases for rest and celebration. **AHLB:** 2812 (N) **Strong's:** 7676

933. שָׂדֶה / [illegible] / sa-deh **Translation:** Field **Definition:** An open land area free of trees and buildings. A level plot of ground. **AHLB:** 1326-H (N) **Strong's:** 7704

934. שַׁדַּי / [illegible] / shad-dai **Translation:** Shaddai **Definition:** A name of YHWH literally meaning "my breasts." **AHLB:** 1464-A (N) **Strong's:** 7706

935. שֶׂה / [illegible] / seh **Translation:** Ram **Definition:** A member of a flock of sheep or goats. **AHLB:** 1327-A (N) **Strong's:** 7716

936. שָׁוְא / [illegible] / sha-weh **Translation:** Falseness **Definition:** Words or actions that are not true or are empty. A Deception. Lacking value and content. **AHLB:** 1461-J (N) **Strong's:** 7723

937. שׁוֹעֵר / [illegible] / sho-eyr **Translation:** Gatekeeper **Definition:** One who guards the gate of a city or the door of a structure. **AHLB:** 2862 (g) **Strong's:** 7778

938. שׁוֹפָר / [illegible] / sho-phar **Translation:** Ram horn **Definition:** The horn of ram made into a trumpet that emits a bright and beautiful sound. **AHLB:** 2869 (g) **Strong's:** 7782

939. שׁוֹר / [illegible] / shor **Translation:** Ox **Definition:** A domestic bovine animal used for pulling heavy loads. **AHLB:** 1480-J (N) **Strong's:** 7794

940. שִׁטָּה / [illegible] / shit-tah **Translation:** Acacia **Definition:** A thorny tree commonly found in the Near East. In its plural form can mean wood or boards from the tree. **AHLB:** 1469-A (N1) **Strong's:** 7848

941. שָׂטָן / [illegible] / sa-tan **Translation:** Opponent **Definition:** One who is on the opposing side of an action or thought; an adversary. **AHLB:** 2475 (N) **Strong's:** 7854

942. שִׁיר / shir **Translation:** Song **Definition:** The act or art of singing. **AHLB:** 1480-M (N) **Strong's:** 7892

943. שָׂכָר / sa-khar **Translation:** Wage **Definition:** The reward or price paid for one's labor. **AHLB:** 2479 (N) **Strong's:** 7939

944. שָׁלוֹם / sha-lom **Translation:** Completeness **Definition:** Something that has been finished or made whole. A state of being complete. **AHLB:** 2845 (c) **Strong's:** 7965

More about the word שָׁלוֹם

When we hear the word peace, which this word is usually translated as, we usually associate this to mean an absence of war or strife. However, the Hebrew word shalom has a very different meaning. The verb form of the root word is shalam and is usually used in the context of making restitution. When a person has caused another to become deficient in some way, such as a loss of livestock, it is the responsibility of the person who created the deficiency to restore what has been taken, lost or stolen. The verb shalam literally means to make whole or complete. The noun shalom has the more literal meaning of being in a state of wholeness, or being without deficiency. The Biblical phrase "shalu shalom yerushalayim" (pray for the peace of Jerusalem) is not speaking about an absence of war (though that is part of it), but that Jerusalem, and by extension all of Israel, be complete and whole and goes far beyond the idea of "peace".

945. שֻׁלְחָן / / shul-hhan **Translation:** Table **Definition:** A flat surface, usually made of wood and with four legs, for laying out the meal to be eaten. **AHLB:** 2842 (om) **Strong's:** 7979

946. שָׁלָל / / sha-lal **Translation:** Spoil **Definition:** Plunder taken from an enemy in war or robbery. To impair the quality or effect of. **AHLB:** 1472-B (N) **Strong's:** 7998

947. שֶׁלֶם / / she-lem **Translation:** Peace offering **Definition:** A sacrifice or offering given to bring about peace. **AHLB:** 2845 (N) **Strong's:** 8002

948. שָׁלֵם / / sha-leym **Translation:** Complete **Definition:** Having all necessary parts, elements or steps. A state of being whole or full. Left unaltered and whole in its original functional state without removing or adding to it. To finish. **AHLB:** 2845 (N) **Strong's:** 8003

949. שִׁלְשׁוֹם / / shil-shom **Translation:** Three days ago **Definition:** Literally the day before yesterday, but used as an idiom for the past. **AHLB:** 2847 (eqp) **Strong's:** 8032

950. שֵׁם / / sheym **Translation:** Title **Definition:** A word given to an individual or place denoting its character. The character of an individual or place. **AHLB:** 1473-A (N) **Strong's:** 8034

More about the word שֵׁם

When we see a name, such as "King David" we see the word "King" as a title and "David" as a name. In our western mind a title describes a character trait while a name is simply an identifier. In the Hebrew language there is no such distinction between names and titles. Both words, King and David, are descriptions of character traits. The Hebrew word melekh (king) is "one who reigns," while daviyd (David) is "one who is loved". Both of these words are titles, describing the character of David. It is also common to identify the word "Elohiym" (Elohiym) as a title and YHWH (Yahweh) as a name. What we do not realize is that both of these are character traits. YHWH is both a word and title meaning "one who exists" and Elohiym is a word and a title meaning "one who has power and authority". The Hebrew word "shem" more literally means "character". When the Bible speaks of taking Elohiym's name to the nations, he is not speaking about the name itself but his character. When we are commanded to not take Elohiym's name in vain, this literally means not to represent his character in a false manner. This is similar to our expression, "have a good name," which is not about the name itself but the character of the one with that name.

951. שַׁמָּה / [illegible] / sha-mah **Translation:** Desolate **Definition:** A wind blowing over the land pulls the moisture out of the ground drying it up, making a place of ruin or desert. **AHLB:** 1473-A (N1) **Strong's:** 8047

952. שְׂמוֹאל / / s-mol **Translation:** Left hand **Definition:** The left hand, side or direction. **AHLB:** 3036 **Strong's:** 8040

953. שְׁמוּעָה / / sh-mu-ah **Translation:** Report **Definition:** News or tidings given to another. **AHLB:** 2851 (d1) **Strong's:** 8052

954. שִׂמְחָה / / sim-hhah **Translation:** Joy **Definition:** A state of felicity or happiness. **AHLB:** 2487 (N1) **Strong's:** 8057

955. שָׁמַיִם / / sha-ma-yim **Translation:** Sky **Definition:** The upper atmosphere that constitutes an apparent great vault or arch over the earth. Place of the winds. **AHLB:** 1473-A (N) **Strong's:** 8064

956. שִׂמְלָה / / sim-lah **Translation:** Apparel **Definition:** Something that clothes or adorns. As forming to the image of the body. **AHLB:** 2489 (e1) **Strong's:** 8071

957. שְׁמָמָה / / sh-ma-mah **Translation:** Desolate **Definition:** Vacant or void of required sources for life. **AHLB:** 1473-B (N1) **Strong's:** 8077

958. שֶׁמֶן / / she-men **Translation:** Oil **Definition:** A semi-liquid, often oily and thick. Usually olive oil and used as a medicinal ointment. Also, meaning fat or rich. **AHLB:** 2850 (N) **Strong's:** 8081

959. שֶׁמֶשׁ / 𐤔𐤌𐤔 / she-mesh **Translation:** Sun **Definition:** The luminous body around which the earth revolves and from which it receives heat and light. **AHLB:** 2854 (N) **Strong's:** 8121

960. שֵׁן / 𐤔𐤍 / sheyn **Translation:** Tooth **Definition:** Hard bony appendages on the jaws used for chewing food and forming of sounds when talking. **AHLB:** 1474-A (N) **Strong's:** 8127

961. שָׁנֵה / 𐤔𐤍𐤄 / sha-neyh **Translation:** Year **Definition:** The period of around 365 solar days. **AHLB:** 1474-A (N1) **Strong's:** 8141

962. שָׁנִי / 𐤔𐤍𐤉 / sha-ni **Translation:** Scarlet **Definition:** Any of various bright reds. **AHLB:** 1474-A (f) **Strong's:** 8144

963. שָׂעִיר / 𐤔𐤏𐤉𐤓 / sa-ir **Translation:** Goat **Definition:** Related to the sheep but of lighter build and with backwardly arching horns, a short tail, and usually straight hair. **AHLB:** 2494 (b) **Strong's:** 8163

964. שַׁעַר / 𐤔𐤏𐤓 / sha-ar **Translation:** Gate **Definition:** The opening in a wall or fence through which livestock or people pass. May also mean a gatekeeper. Also sha'ar, a unit of measurement. **AHLB:** 2862 (N) **Strong's:** 8179

965. שֵׂעָר / 𐤔𐤏𐤓 / sey-ar **Translation:** Hair **Definition:** The covering of filaments on a human head or the body of an animal. **AHLB:** 2494 (N) **Strong's:** 8181

966. שְׂעֹרָה / 𐤔𐤏𐤅𐤓𐤄 / s-o-rah **Translation:** Barley **Definition:** A crop used as food, and for determining the month of Aviv. **AHLB:** 2494 (c1) **Strong's:** 8184

967. שָׂפָה / / sa-phah **Translation:** Lip **Definition:** The rim or edge of the mouth or other opening. Language, as spoken from the lips. **AHLB:** 1339-A (N1) **Strong's:** 8193

968. שִׁפְחָה / / shiph-hhah **Translation:** Maid **Definition:** An unmarried young woman. **AHLB:** 2863 (e1) **Strong's:** 8198

969. שַׂק / / saq **Translation:** Sack **Definition:** A bag of cloth or skins for carrying foods or objects. **AHLB:** 1341-A (N) **Strong's:** 8242

970. שִׁקּוּץ / / shi-quts **Translation:** Filthiness **Definition:** A dirty, shameful, or detestable action, object or condition. Often used in the context of idols. **AHLB:** 2878 (ed) **Strong's:** 8251

971. שֶׁקֶל / / she-qel **Translation:** Sheqel **Definition:** A chief Hebrew weight standard of measurement. **AHLB:** 2874 (N) **Strong's:** 8255

972. שֶׁקֶר / / she-qer **Translation:** False **Definition:** A deliberate lie. An expression of a non-truth. **AHLB:** 2879 (N) **Strong's:** 8267

973. שַׂר / / sar **Translation:** Noble **Definition:** Possessing outstanding qualities or properties. Of high birth or exalted rank. One who has authority. May also mean "heavy" from the weight of responsibility on one in authority. **AHLB:** 1342-A (N) **Strong's:** 8269

974. שָׂרִיד / / sa-rid **Translation:** Remnant **Definition:** What is left behind. **AHLB:** 2506 (b) **Strong's:** 8300

975. שֹׁרֶשׁ / ⵡⴽⴰⵅⵡ / sho-resh **Translation:** Root **Definition:** The underground part of a plant. The source or origin of a thing. **AHLB:** 2883 (g) **Strong's:** 8328

976. שֵׁשׁ / ⵡⵡ / sheysh **Translation:** Linen **Definition:** Fabric made of flax and noted for its strength, coolness and luster. A white cloth. Also, marble from its whiteness. **AHLB:** 1481-A (N) **Strong's:** 8336

Tav

977. תְּאֵן / ⵏⴷ+ / t-eyn **Translation:** Fig **Definition:** An oblong or pear-shaped fruit from a tree of the fichus genus. **AHLB:** 1014-A (i) **Strong's:** 8384

978. תֵּבָה / ⵜⵎ+ / tey-vah **Translation:** Vessel **Definition:** A floating container for holding items. Used for the basket that carried Mosheh down the Nile river and the boat made by Noah. **AHLB:** 1028-A (i) **Strong's:** 8392

979. תְּבוּאָה / ⵜⴷⵅⵎ+ / t-vu-ah **Translation:** Production **Definition:** Total output of a commodity or an industry. An increase of produce, usually of fruit. **AHLB:** 1024-J (i1) **Strong's:** 8393

980. תֵּבֵל / ⵍⵎ+ / tey-vel **Translation:** Earth **Definition:** The whole of the land or region. **AHLB:** 1035-A (i) **Strong's:** 8398

981. תְּהוֹם / ⵎⵅⵜ+ / t-hom **Translation:** Deep sea **Definition:** Extending far from some surface or area; in difficulty or distress. Deep and tumultuous water. A subterranean body of water. **AHLB:** 1105-J (i) **Strong's:** 8415

982. תְּהִלָּה / / t-hi-lah **Translation:** Adoration **Definition:** To praise or to be boastful. **AHLB:** 1104-A (ie1) **Strong's:** 8416

983. תּוֹדָה / / to-dah **Translation:** Thanks **Definition:** An expression of gratitude or acknowledgement toward another. **AHLB:** 1211-A (i1) **Strong's:** 8426

984. תָּוֶךְ / / ta-wek **Translation:** Midst **Definition:** The center or middle of the whole. **AHLB:** 1494-J (N) **Strong's:** 8432

985. תּוֹכֵחָה / / to-khey-hhah **Translation:** Conviction **Definition:** A fixed or firm confidence in truth. **AHLB:** 1238-L (i1) **Strong's:** 8433

986. תּוֹלְדָה / / tol-dah **Translation:** Birthing **Definition:** The act or process of bringing forth offspring from the womb. Total of the children born within an era. **AHLB:** 1257-L (i3) **Strong's:** 8435

987. תּוֹלָע / / to-la **Translation:** Kermes **Definition:** The 'coccus ilicis,' a worm used for medicinal purposes as well as for making a crimson dye. **AHLB:** 1269-L (i) **Strong's:** 8438

988. תּוֹעֵבָה / / to-ey-vah **Translation:** Disgusting **Definition:** Something highly distasteful that arouses marked aversion in one. **AHLB:** 2897 (g1) **Strong's:** 8441

989. תּוֹרָה / 𐤕𐤅𐤓𐤄 / to-rah **Translation:** Teaching **Definition:** Acquired knowledge or skills that mark the direction one is to take in life. A straight direction. Knowledge passed from one person to another. **AHLB:** 1227-H (i1) **Strong's:** 8451

More about the word תּוֹרָה

To interpret the Hebrew word torah as law is about the same as interpreting the word father as disciplinarian. While the father is a disciplinarian he is much more and in the same way torah is much more than law. The word torah is derived from the root yarah meaning to throw. This can be the throwing of a rock, the shooting of an arrow, or the pointing of the finger to show direction. Another word derived from this root is the word moreh, which can mean and archer, one who throws the arrow, or a teacher, as one who points the way. The word torah is literally the teachings of the teacher or parent. When a parent is teaching a child a new task and he demonstrates a willingness to learn, but fails to grasp the teaching completely, the parent does not punish the child, but rather encourages him. In contrast to this, a law is a set of rules that if not observed correctly, will result in punishment, and there is no room for teaching. The torah of Elohiym are his teachings to his children which are given in love to encourage and strengthen.

990. תִּירוֹשׁ / 𐤕𐤉𐤓𐤅𐤔 / ti-rosh **Translation:** Fresh wine **Definition:** Newly pressed wine as a desired possession. **AHLB:** 1458-L (ic) **Strong's:** 8492

991. תְּכֵלֶת / / t-khey-let **Translation:** Blue **Definition:** A color that is created with the use of a dye. **AHLB:** 1242-A (i2) **Strong's:** 8504

992. תָּמִיד / / ta-mid **Translation:** Continually **Definition:** Happening without interruption or cessation; continuous in time. **AHLB:** 1280-M (b) **Strong's:** 8548

993. תָּמִים / / ta-mim **Translation:** Whole **Definition:** Free of wound or injury; free of defect or impairment; having all its proper parts or components. **AHLB:** 1496-B (b) **Strong's:** 8549

994. תְּנוּפָה / / t-nu-phah **Translation:** Waving **Definition:** The action of moving an object, such as hammer or a sacrifice, back and forth. **AHLB:** 1316-J (i1) **Strong's:** 8573

995. תִּפְאָרָה / / tiph-a-rah **Translation:** Decoration **Definition:** Ornamentation that shows position or distinction. **AHLB:** 1388-D (i1) **Strong's:** 8597

996. תְּפִלָּה / / t-phi-lah **Translation:** Pleading **Definition:** To earnestly appeal to another for or against an action. **AHLB:** 1380-M (i1) **Strong's:** 8605

997. תִּקְוָה / / tiq-wah **Translation:** Waiting **Definition:** A standing still in anticipation or expectation. **AHLB:** 1420-A (i1) **Strong's:** 8615

998. תְּרוּמָה / / t-ru-mah **Translation:** Offering **Definition:** A donation presented to another. **AHLB:** 1450-J (i1) **Strong's:** 8641

999. תְּרוּעָה / 𐤕𐤓𐤅𐤏𐤄 / t-ru-ah **Translation:** Shout **Definition:** A great shout of alarm of war or for rejoicing. **AHLB:** 1460-J (i1) **Strong's:** 8643

1000. תְּשׁוּעָה / 𐤕𐤔𐤅𐤏𐤄 / t-shu-ah **Translation:** Rescue **Definition:** A deliverance or freedom from a burden, enemy or trouble. **AHLB:** 1476-L (i1) **Strong's:** 8668

Appendix A ~ The Alphabet

Name	Modern		Ancient	
Aleph	א	silent		ah, eh
Beyt/Veyt	בּ ב	b, v		b, v
Gimel	ג	g		g
Dalet	ד	d		d
Hey	ה	h		h, ey
Vav	ו וּ וֹ	v, o, u	Y	w, ow, uw
Zayin	ז	z		z
Hhet	ח	hh[1]		hh*
Thet	ט	t	⊗	t
Yud	י	y		y, iy
Kaph/Khaph	כּ כ ך ךּ	k, kh[1]		k, kh
Lamed	ל	l		l
Mem	מ ם	m		m
Nun	נ ן	n		n
Samehh	ס	s		s
Ayin	ע	silent	/	ah / gh
Pey/Phey	פּ פ ף	p, ph		p, ph
Tsade	צ ץ	ts		ts
Quph	ק	q		q
Resh	ר	r		r
Shin/Sin	שׁ שׂ	sh, s		sh
Tav	ת	t	+	t

[1] Pronounced hard, like the "ch" in the name Bach.

The Vowels

אָ[2]	Qamats	a, as in father
אַ	Patahh	a, as in father
אֶ	Segol	e, as in egg
אֵ	Tsere	ey, as in grey
אְ	Sh'va	silent
אִ	Hhireq	i, as in machine
אֹ	Hholam	o, as in row
אֻ	Qubbuts	u, as in tune
אֳ	Hhataph Qamats	a, as in father
אֲ	Hhataph Patahh	a, as in father
אֱ	Hhataph Segol	e, as in egg
וֹ	Hholam Maley	o, as in row
וּ	Shurruq	u, as in tune

[2] The letter "aleph" is used to show the placement of the vowel pointing and is not part of the vowel.

Appendix B ~ Prefixes and Suffixes

The Prefixes

Six letters are frequently prefixed to nouns and verbs. Below are these six letters and examples of their uses.

The prefix ב (b) is the preposition meaning "within" and is usually translated as "in" or with."

#666	במדבר	bamidbar	in *the* wilderness
#573	בחרב	behharev	with *the* sword
#352	בשלח	b'shalahh	in *the* send*ing*

The prefix ל (l) is the preposition meaning "toward" and is usually translated as "to" or "for."

#440	לארץ	la'arets	to *the* land
#464	לבן	l'veyn	to/for *a* son
#121	לדעה	l'deyah	to know

Appendix B ~ Prefixes and Suffixes

The prefix מ (m) is the preposition meaning "from."

#459	מבית	mibeyt	from *the* house
#592	מיד	miyad	from *the* hand

The prefix כ (k) is the preposition meaning "like."

#415	כאלהים	keylohim	like *the* powers
#624	ככל	k'khol	like all

The prefix ו (v/u) is the conjunction meaning "and."

#498	וגר	v'geyr	and *a* stranger
#503	ודבש	ud'vash	and honey
#197	ונגע	un'go'a	and touch

The prefix ה (h) is the article meaning "the."

#506	הדור	hador	the generation
#585	הטוב	hatov	the functional *one*
#24	הבא	haba	the com*ing*

The Suffixes (Possessive Pronouns)

Nouns are frequently suffixed by a letter (or letters) representing a pronoun. This noun/pronoun combination is in the construct state (identified in English with the word "of"). An example of a Hebrew construct state is ביתי (beytiy) which would literally be translated as "house of me," but would normally be translated as "my house."

ביתי	bey'tiy	my house
ביתך	bey'te'kha	your (mas) house
ביתך	bey'teykh	your (fem) house
ביתו	bey'to	his house
ביתה	bey'tah	her house
ביתנו	bey'tey'nu	our house
ביתכם	bey'te'khem	your (mas, pl) house
ביתכן	bey'te'khen	your (fem, pl) house
ביתם	bey'tam	their(mas) house
ביתן	bey'tan	their (fem) house

The Suffixes (Plurals)

Nouns are made plural by adding a suffix, either ים (im) for masculine nouns or ות (ot) for feminine nouns. There are a few exceptions to this though. For instance, the Hebrew word

אב (father) is a masculine noun but in the plural is written as אבות (avot). Below are a few examples of Hebrew plurals.

#464	בנים	beniym	sons
#477	בנות	banot	daughters
#594	ימים	yamim	days
#397	אתות	otot	signs

Combinations

והארץ v'ha'arets	The prefix ו meaning "and" The prefix ה meaning "the" The word ארץ meaning "land" and the land
מידו mi'ya'do	The prefix מ meaning "from" The word יד meaning "hand" The suffix ו meaning "his" from his hand
לנו lanu	The prefix ל meaning "to" The suffix נו meaning "us"

	To us
בניכם b'ney'khem	The word בן meaning "son" The masc. plural suffix ים [3] The suffix כם meaning "you" (mas, pl) **your sons**

[3] When a masculine plural word is written in the construct state, the letter ם (m) is dropped.

Appendix C ~ Pronouns, Prepositions, Etc.

Pronouns

אֲנִי	a'ni	I
אָנֹכִי	a'no'khi	I
אֲנוּ	a'nu	We
אֲנַחְנוּ	a'nahh'nu	We
אַתָּה	a'tah	You (mas, sing)
אַתְּ	at	You (fem, sing)
אַתֶּם	a'tem	You (mas, plural)
אַתֶּן	a'ten	You (fem, plural)
הוּא	hu	He
הִיא	hi	She
הֵם	heym	They (mas)
הֵן	heyn	They (fem)

Indefinite Pronouns

זֹאת	zot	This (fem)
זֶה	zeh	This (mas)
אֵלֶּה	ey'leh	These

Prepositions

אֵל	eyl	To, For
אִם	im	If
בֵּין	beyn	Between
כִּי	ki	Because, For
מִין	min	From
עַד	ad	Until
עוֹד	od	Again
עַל	al	Upon, Over
שָׁם	sham	There
עִם	im	With

Adverbs

כֵּן	keyn	So
עַתָּה	a'tah	Now
אַךְ	ak	Indeed, Surely
רַק	raq	Only
אוּלַי	u'lai	Perhaps
אוּלָם	u'lam	But
אַיִן	ain	Without

Conjunctions

אֲשֶׁר	a'sheyr	Which
אוֹ	o	Or
גַּם	gam	Also
פֶּן	pen	Otherwise

Other

אֵת [4]	eyt	At
לוֹא [5]	lo	Not

[4] The Hebrew word אֵת precedes the definite object of the verb. For instance, in the sentence, "John drove the car," The words "the car" are the definite object and in Hebrew these words would be proceeded by the word אֵת. Here is a Biblical example from Genesis 1:4, וַיַּרְא אֱלֹהִים אֶת הָאוֹר, which is translated as "and Elohiym saw אֵת the light."

[5] The word לוֹא (usually written as לֹא) precedes a verb to negate the action of that verb. An example can be found in Genesis 2:17, which includes the phrase לֹא תֹאכַל. The word תֹאכַל (tokhal) means, "you will eat," but because it is preceded by the word לֹא, it means "you will not eat."

Appendix D ~ Numbers

Cardinal Numbers

אֶחָד	e'hhad	One (mas)
אַחַת	a'hhat	One (fem)
שְׁנַיִם	sh'na'yim	Two (mas)
שְׁתַּיִם	sh'ta'yim	Two (fem)
שְׁלֹשָׁה	sh'lo'shah	Three (mas)
שָׁלוֹשׁ	sha'losh	Three (fem)
אַרְבָּעָה	ar'ba'ah	Four (mas)
אַרְבַּע	ar'ba	Four (fem)
חֲמִשָּׁה	hha'mi'shah	Five (mas)
חָמֵשׁ	hha'meysh	Five (fem)
שִׁשָּׁה	shi'shah	Six (mas)
שֵׁשׁ	sheysh	Six (fem)
שִׁבְעָה	shiv'ah	Seven (mas)
שֶׁבַע	sh'va	Seven (fem)
שְׁמֹנָה	sh'mo'nah	Eight (mas)
שְׁמֹנֶה	sh'mo'neh	Eight (fem)
תִּשְׁעָה	tish'ah	Nine (mas)
תֵּשַׁע	t'sha	Nine (fem)

Appendix D ~ Numbers

עֲשָׂרָה	a'sa'rah	Ten (mas)
עֶשֶׂר	e'ser	Ten (fem)
עֶשְׂרִים	es'rim	Twenty
שְׁלוֹשִׁים	sh'lo'shim	Thirty
אַרְבָּעִים	ar'ba'im	Forty
חֲמִשִׁים	hha'mi'shim	Fifty
שִׁשִׁים	shi'shim	Sixty
שִׁבְעִים	shiv'im	Seventy
שְׁמֹנִים	sh'mo'nim	Eighty
תִּשְׁעִים	tish'im	Ninety
מֵאָה	mey'ah	Hundred
אֶלֶף	e'leph	Thousand

Ordinal Numbers

רִאשׁוֹן	ri'shon	First (mas)
רִאשֹׁנָה	ri'sho'nah	First (fem)
שֵׁנִי	shey'ni	Second (mas)
שֵׁנִית	shey'nit	Second (fem)
שְׁלִישִׁי	sh'li'shi	Third (mas)
שְׁלִישִׁית	sh'li'shit	Third (fem)
רְבִיעִי	r'vi'i	Fourth (mas)
רְבִיעִית	r'vi'it	Fourth (fem)
חֲמִישִׁי	hha'mi'shi	Fifth (mas)
חֲמִישִׁית	hha'mi'shit	Fifth (fem)
שִׁישִׁי	shi'shi	Sixth (mas)
שִׁישִׁית	shi'shit	Sixth (fem)
שְׁבִיעִי	sh'vi'i	Seventh (mas)
שְׁבִיעִית	sh'vi'it	Seventh (fem)
שְׁמִינִי	sh'mi'ni	Eighth (mas)
שְׁמִינִית	sh'mi'nit	Eighth (fem)
תְּשִׁיעִי	t'shi'i	Ninth (mas)
תְּשִׁיעִית	t'shi'it	Ninth (fem)
עֲשִׂירִי	a'si'ri	Tenth (mas)
עֲשִׂירִת	a'si'rit	Tenth (fem)

Appendix E ~ Verb Conjugations

Tense and Subject

Most conjugated Hebrew verbs identify the tense of the verb and the gender and number of the subject of the verb.

Hebrew verb tenses are not related to time (past, present or future), as in English, but to action. There are two Hebrew tenses; perfect and imperfect. The perfect tense is used for a complete action and is usually translated with the English past tense. The imperfect tense is used for an incomplete action (an action that has started but not finished or an action that has not started) and is usually translated with the English present or future tense.

The tense and the subject of the verb are identified by a prefix and/or suffix attached to the verb. While there are many different combinations of verb conjugations, a few common examples using the verb קצר (#301) are provided below.

קצרתי	qa'tsar'ti	I cut
קצרנו	qa'tsar'nu	We cut
קצרת	qa'tsar'ta	You cut
קצר	qa'tsar	He cut
קצרו	qats'ru	They cut

קצרה	qats'rah	She cut
אקצר	eq'tsor	I will cut
נקצר	niq'tsor	We will cut
תקצר	tiq'tsor	You will cut
יקצר	yi'qe'tsor	He will cut
יקצרו	yi'qe'tse'ru	They will cut
תקצר	ti'qe'tsor	She will cut

The Reversing Vav

When the letter vav (ו), meaning "and," is prefixed to a verb, it usually reverses the tense of the verb. For instance, the verb יקצר means "he will cut," but when written as ויקצר, it means "and he cut."

Index ~ By Translation

Index ~ By Translation

Index ~ By Translation

Index ~ By Translation

Index ~ By Translation

Index ~ By Translation

Index ~ By Strong's

Index ~ By Strong's

Index ~ By Strong's

Index ~ By Strong's

Index ~ By Strong's

CPSIA information can be obtained
at www.ICGtesting.com
Printed in the USA
BVHW031556280319
543877BV00002B/91/P